Mini Rex Rat

Mini Rex Rabbits Pets

Mini Rex Rabbits book for care, housing, keeping, diet, training and health.

By

Macy Peterson

Table of Contents

Introduction

I want to thank you and congratulate you for buying the book 'Mini Rex Rabbit as a pet'. This book will help you to understand everything you need to know about domesticating a Mini Rex Rabbit. You will learn all the aspects related to raising the Mini Rex Rabbit successfully at home. You will be able to understand the pros and cons, behaviour, breeding, basic care, keeping, housing, diet and health issues related to the animal.

Rabbits have always been an owner's dream. They are friendly, calm and they look beautiful. Everybody is impressed by the adorable looks of the rabbits. People think that the good looks of the rabbit are a good enough reason to domesticate the animal. But, domestication of a bunny has its unique challenges and issues. It is important to understand these challenges.

If you wish to domesticate a Mini Rex Rabbit, then you should understand the various breeds of the Mini Rex Rabbit. This will help you to make a better choice. If you are not ready for the challenges that await you as the caregiver of the Mini Rex Rabbit, then you are not ready to domesticate the animal.

If you have already bought or adopted a Mini Rex Rabbit, even then you need to understand your pet so that you take care of him in a better way. It is important that you understand that owning any pet will have its advantages and disadvantages. You should see whether with all its pros and cons, the animal fits well into your household. Domesticating and taming a pet is not only fun. There is a lot of hard work that goes into it.

When you bring a pet home, it becomes your responsibility to raise the pet in the best way possible. You have to provide physically, mentally, emotionally and financially for the pet.

It should be noted that whether you keep a Mini Rex Rabbit for its invaluable wool or only as a friendly pet in the house, you will have to dedicate a lot of time to the animal. The animal will depend on you for its food and shelter needs. As the owner and the parent, it is your responsibility to make sure that you provide optimum conditions for the good well-being of your pet.

The Mini Rex will need a lot of love and care from your side. Like most pet animals, the Mini Rex Rabbit is also prone to various kinds of diseases. As the owner and caregiver, you should attempt to understand these diseases in detail, so that you can provide the pet bunny with the right care.

When you are looking to maintain the health of your pet Mini Rex Rabbit, then you should make an attempt to understand the common health issues that the animal faces. This will help you to prepare yourself well and also treat your pet well.

It is very important that you take time to understand the various stages in the pet's life. Each stage will demand for different care and methods. So when you get the Mini Rex Rabbit home, you should make sure that you understand the needs of the animal at various stages of his life.

It is important that you are ready to commit before you decide to domesticate the animal. If you are a prospective buyer, then understanding of these points will help you to make a wise decision. Before you embark on this journey of raising your pet, it is important to evaluate your resources and make sure that you are ready for the pet.

You should also evaluate the practical side of things. It is important that you know that the cost of bringing up a Mini Rex Rabbit might be more than the cost you would have to encounter while raising a dog or a cat.

A pet is like a family member. This is the basic requirement to domesticate an animal. It is more than important that you take care of all the responsibilities of the animal.

It is important to have a thorough understanding about the animal. Spend some time to know everything about the Mini Rex Rabbit. This will help you know your pet better. The more you know about your pet, the better bond you will form with him. Whenever you get a pet home, you have to make sure that you are all ready for the responsibilities ahead.

If you wish to raise a Mini Rex Rabbit as a pet, there are many things that you need to keep in mind. Because of the lack of information, you will find yourself getting confused as to what should be done and what should be avoided. You might be confused and scared. But, there is no need to feel so confused. After you learn about the Mini Rex Rabbits, you will know how adorable they are. You should equip yourself with the right knowledge.

It is important that you understand the basic behaviour of the Mini Rex Rabbit. This will help you to understand what lies ahead of you. If you understand how a rabbit should be cared for, you will make it work for yourself. You should aim at learning about the animal and then doing the right thing for him. This will help you to form a relationship with him.

Once you form a relationship with the Mini Rex Rabbit, it gets better and easier for you as the caregiver. The pet will grow up to be friendly and adorable. He will also value the bond as much as you do. This will be good for the pet and also for you as the pet caregiver in the long run.

If you are looking to domesticate the Mini Rex Rabbit, then you might be having many questions and doubts. You still might not be sure whether you want to buy the bunny or not. If you are still doubtful, then this book is meant to help you make a well-informed decision. You should objectively look at the various advantages and disadvantages of owning a Mini Rex Rabbit. This will help you to make your decision.

Mini Rex Rabbits can grow up to be very good and lovable pets if they are loved and cared for in the beginning. Their first year is a crucial time because this is when the kit forms intimate bonds with human beings. The emotional bonds that it forms at this stage will stay with him for his life. He will be loyal towards them. Make sure that you pay as much attention to the development of the baby bunny.

This book is meant to equip you with all the knowledge that you need to have for successful domestication of a Mini Rex Rabbit. This book will help you understand the basic behaviour and antics of the animal. You will also learn of various tricks and tips. These tips and tricks will be a quick guide when you are looking for different ways to have fun with your pet. It is important that a prospective buyer has all the important information regarding the animal.

This book will help you in the preparation being a good caregiver and a better owner for your pet. You will learn many ways to take care of your pet animal. This book will try to address every question that you might have when looking at raising the Mini Rex Rabbit.

You can expect to learn the pet's basic behaviour, eating habits, shelter requirements, breeding, grooming and training techniques among other important things. The book will help you to be a better owner by learning everything about the animal. This will help you form an everlasting bond with the pet.

Chapter 1: Understanding Mini Rex Rabbits

Rabbits have always been a popular choice for pet enthusiasts around the world. People love rabbits for their playfulness and also their cute looks. There are many breeds of rabbits. The different breeds are popular for different reasons.

Mini Rex Rabbit is a very popular domestic breed of rabbits. While this type of rabbit is obviously popular for its cute looks, it is also popular for another important reason. The Mini Rex Rabbit is widely known for its fur.

The fur of the Mini Rex Rabbit is very smooth, soft and gorgeous. This is one of the most unique features of the animal. This makes the animal a popular choice with the fibre enthusiasts and artists and also the rabbit lovers. It should be noted here that the wool derived from the Mini Rex's skin is priced at a high value. It is an item of luxury owned by wool enthusiasts. It is said to be of a better quality than even the sheep's wool.

The Mini Rex Rabbits require a great deal of grooming from its owner. This is because the wool of the pet is very thick. If you don't groom the pet every day, the wool can get entangled and the pet can acquire various problems.

The Mini Rex wool is very soft and also very warm. It is almost seven times warmer than high quality sheep wool. The structural network of the fibres in the wool provides it the much needed thermal quality. Mini Rex yarn and Mini Rex warm garments are very popular for the same reason.

1. Origin of the Mini Rex Rabbit

The exact origin of the Mini Rex Rabbit is still a topic of debate for the Mini Rex Rabbit enthusiasts. But, it is believed that the presence of large rabbits was found even in the eighteenth century.

The present age Mini Rex Rabbits have descended from a breed of rabbit that was Turkish in its origin. This breed was used for its wool.

Some sailors from Yore loved the quality of the wool of these rabbits. They found it to be useful and so decided to take some of these rabbits back with them to France. The rabbits became very popular after that in France.

It is also known that the Mini Rex Rabbits came to the United States of America in the first half of the next century, i.e. nineteenth century. Mini Rex was the common name of all the breeds of the Mini Rex at particular time.

Mini Rex is known to be a very popular breed of domestic bunnies that was created in the year 1984. This was done in Texas. It should also be noted that many Mini Rex clubs exist all around the world. These Mini Rex Rabbit clubs have dedicated themselves to the preservation and care of these beautiful Mini Rex Rabbits.

The National Mini Rex Rabbits Breeders club is one such club that has dedicated itself to the care of Mini Rex Rabbits. It is the national club for the main four breeds of the Mini Rex Rabbits.

2. Harvesting of wool

The Mini Rex Rabbits are very popular for the quality and quantity of the wool they shed. It is known that the harvesting of the Agora wool is very popular. The harvesting of the wool is also very simple.

You can harvest the wool of the Mini Rex Rabbit by the process of shearing or by the process of plucking. Both these processes are equally popular. Though the process if simple, each breed of the Mini Rex will have certain details of harvesting that are specific to it.

If you are interested in the harvesting of Mini Rex wool, then it is better if you can take the guidance of an experienced breeder.

3. Life span of Mini Rex Rabbits

A healthy Mini Rex Rabbit can live from 7 to over 12 years. It is known that a Mini Rex Rabbit that is cared for and groomed in a good way and that is kept indoors will have a good life span. The key is to provide them the right environment and also the right nutrition. This will help them to grow, stay healthy and live longer.

4. Size, weight and colour

The size and weight of the bunny (rabbit) will depend on the breed of the Mini Rex Rabbit. The typical Giant Mini Rex Rabbit will weigh about ten pounds. The Jersey is the smallest of all the breeds of the Mini Rex Rabbit. A mature bunny of this breed will weigh about 3.5 pounds.

The Giant Mini Rex male rabbit can weigh over 12 pounds. It is known that the female in this breed can weigh more than the male. The English Mini Rex Rabbit weighs 5-7 pounds. The French Mini Rex Rabbit weighs 7-11 pounds.

ARBA recognizes an assortment of the various rainbow colours of Satin Mini Rex Rabbit, French Mini Rex Rabbit and English Mini Rex Rabbit. An owner can decide to show these breeds of Mini Rex Rabbits also. These colours include blue eyed white, opal, chocolate, lynx, fawn, red and sable.

Satin Mini Rex Rabbit and French Mini Rex Rabbit can also be in Siamese smoke pearl. French Mini Rex Rabbit can be in a broken colour pattern.

ARBA recognizes the Giant Mini Rex breed only in one colour, which is the beautiful ruby eyed white. This is the only colour the Giant Mini Rex Rabbit can be in.

5. Body types of the Mini Rex Rabbits

It is known that different types of Mini Rex Rabbits have different body types and sizes. An idea of these body types will help you to understand the structure of the Mini Rex Rabbits in a better way.

If you wish to learn the various body types of the Mini Rex Rabbits, then the following list will surely help you:

Full arch body type

One of the body types of the Mini Rex Rabbit is the full arch body type. The full arch body type or Mini Rex Rabbits that are very agile and active. They are inclined to be very energetic.

The arch of the rabbit begins at the nape of the neck and continues over the shoulders and the hips in an unbroken and fluid line. This line rounds as it reaches the base of the tail. The ears of the rabbit are erect and the fur is spotted.

The side profile can be visibly seen tapering from the hind quarters to the shoulders. Some of the popular breeds of rabbits possessing this body type are the Rhinelander and English spot.

Semi arch body type

Some of the Mini Rex Rabbits possess the semi arch body type. This body type is also called the gentle giant. This body type represents large bodies of the bunnies.

The shoulders of this body type are lower and the hip is at a higher level. The side profile can be seen to be tapering from hindquarters to the shoulders. Some of the popular breeds of rabbits possessing this body type are the Flemish giant and the American.

Compact Body type

The compact body type Mini Rex Rabbits are smaller in length and are also lighter in weight as compared to the other Mini Rex Rabbits. You can also notice a rise in top line of these bunnies because the depth of shoulders is less than the depth of hips.

They appear to be well balanced in their looks. Some of the compact body type rabbits are the Mini Satin, Mini Lop, the Havana and the Dutch.

Commercial Body type

This body type is used for production and meat. The rabbits with these body types grow very fast in comparison to other body types.

The commercial body type rabbits are equally deep and wide in their appearance. They look similar to the compact body type. They are medium in the length that they attain when they mature.

Some of the commercial body type rabbits are the Rex, the Satin, the Silver Fox, the French Lop and the Giant Mini Rex Rabbit.

Cylindrical Body type

There is only one rabbit breed that is categorised under the cylindrical body type, which is the Himalayan rabbit. The Himalayan rabbit is small in size.

The body of this breed of rabbit is cylindrical and quite similar to the Californian rabbit.

6. Pros and cons of keeping a Mini Rex Rabbit

Domesticating an animal is a very big decision and it is only important that it is taken in the best possible way. You should be well informed when you are trying to make a decision. It is always better to equip yourself with the right information.

If you wish to hand raise an animal, you should make sure that you understand the characteristics and the requirements of the animal well. When you domesticate the Mini Rex Rabbit, you will face many pros and cons on the way.

Take some time to understand the advantages and disadvantages of domesticating the Mini Rex Rabbit, so that you can take a wise decision.

This section will help you understand the pros and cons of keeping a Mini Rex Rabbit at home. No matter which breed of Mini Rex Rabbit you have, you can expect to face the following pros and cons while domesticating the rabbit.

Pros of keeping a Mini Rex Rabbit at home

There are many pros of keeping a Mini Rex Rabbit. The lovable and affectionate animal can prove to be a great companion and pet. Following are the pros of raising the Mini Rex Rabbit at home:

- A Mini Rex Rabbit is a very intelligent and smart animal. You can easily train him to suit your family and living conditions. The rabbit will get accustomed and used to the family very easily and pretty soon.

- The rabbit is beautiful to look at. With its coat wool, it looks like a small ball of fur. If you are fond of beautiful looking pets, then the Mini Rex Rabbit is definitely the pet for you and your family.

- The Mini Rex Rabbits are very energetic and lively pets. They are very active during the early hours of morning and evening.

- These animals can be very social and friendly in their nature. They will get along very well you and your family members.

- Mini Rex Rabbits are known to have fun. They are entertaining, but that does not mean that they will not be calm and gentle. If the pet is supervised well, he will always have fun in certain limits.

- The Mini Rex Rabbits are very sweet and gentle in their nature. But, they need to be trained well so that they don't get too mischievous. You will also get to see the calm, composed and gentle side of the animal.

- An important point to note here is that their nature will depend on how they are raised. If they are raised to be social, they will be very social. So as a master, it will be your responsibility to ensure that the pet gets a healthy and happy upbringing. You should make sure that they spend a lot of time indoors with the family members. This will only help in being more social and affectionate.

- These animals are very funny and entertaining. You can be prepared to have a lot of fun around your Mini Rex Rabbit.

- The Mini Rex Rabbit is a very playful, happy-go-lucky kind of animal. The rabbit likes having fun and can be a constant source of entertainment for everyone in the family. If there are kids in your home, then they will fall in love with this unique animal.

- There are many people who domesticate Mini Rex Rabbits for their warm and exotic wool. If you are a wool enthusiast, then you will love the Mini Rex wool.

- You can enter your pet Mini Rex in various shows that happen everywhere. These are shows that can help you gain popularity and can help you win also.

- If the Mini Rex Rabbit is cared for in the household, they are capable of forming strong emotional bonds. These bonds will last for a life time. You need to spend quality time with your pet to form such strong bonds.

- Mini Rex Rabbits are very calm and composed by nature. They will not create havoc in your home.

- You will find it easier to groom the pet because he will be relaxed and calm, unlike many other pets who don't allow the owners to groom them.

- The rabbit can be used to harvest wool. It should be noted that it is very easy to harvest the wool of the Mini Rex Rabbit and anybody can do it if the proper knowledge of doing it is attained.

- If you show care and concern towards your rabbit, you will only receive love from the animal. The Mini Rex Rabbit will form a very strong emotional bond with you and the other family members.

- It has been established over the years that the Mini Rex Rabbits are easy to train. This can be contrary to what many people might believe.

- When you domesticate a Mini Rex Rabbit, you will have to worry less about his diet. This is because nowadays many diet mixtures and pellets are available commercially. These food items ensure that the right nutrition is given to your beloved pet. And, you can be happy because you can save yourself from the tension of preparing food mixes for the pet every now and then.

- If you happen to rescue a young Mini Rex Rabbit, then the good news is that they can be hand raised. Many a times, when a young animal is rescued, it fails to survive. You would have to be extra careful and cautious while taking care of the kit, but when all the precautions are taken, it is a very much possible task to hand raise a bunny or kit.

- They will respond to the way you choose to communicate with them. If you provide good training to your Mini Rex Rabbit, you will notice that he responds well. In due time and over the course of the training, the pet will also start obeying some simple commands that you would want him to obey.

- These animals are easy to keep. They don't fall sick that often and lead a healthy life.

- They require vaccinations, like most other pet animals do.

- If you have a large number of Mini Rex Rabbits, you can earn a lot of money by harvesting and selling wool.

Cons of keeping a Mini Rex Rabbit at home

There are many cons of keeping a Mini Rex Rabbit. Following are the disadvantages of raising the Mini Rex Rabbit at home:

- Mini Rex Rabbits have the tendency to groom themselves. They will lick themselves like cats. This can cause the bunny to swallow some of the hair or wool. The rabbit is unable to cough this ball of hair, like the cats. This can lead to a serious health issue called the wool block. The hairball remains inside the pet's body in this condition.

This can lead to many complications if the condition is not treated on time.

- If the Mini Rex Rabbit is not under supervision, he can get very mischievous. The animal will chew at things, even electrical wiring. This can pose a danger to him and also others. So, either you should supervise the rabbit or keep him in a place where he does not need supervision and is safe.

- The pet can get stressed and depressed if he is left lonely for longer durations. You can't leave him in the cage for too long.

- The bunnies love to dig in the ground. In fact, the Mini Rex Rabbit will try to dig everywhere. If the pet is left on its own, he might try to dig in your sofas, beds, etc.

- The pet also loves to chew. They can chew away all your furniture and bedding.

- The Mini Rex Rabbit requires a great deal of grooming from its owner. This is because the wool of the pet is very thick. If you don't groom the pet every day, the wool can get entangled and the pet can acquire various problems. If you don't have the time and energy to spend a lot of time of grooming a pet, then the Mini Rex Rabbit is not the right pet for you.

- The Mini Rex Rabbits have the problem of overheating. The body temperature can rise beyond safe limits if proper care is not given. This can happen because of the extremely warm wool of the Mini Rex Rabbit.

- The animal seeks a lot of attention. A Mini Rex Rabbit is a kind of pet that will require you to pamper him a lot.

- The cost that you will incur while buying and raising is more when compared to other pets, such as the dog and the cat.

- If spending too much money is an issue with you, then you will have to think twice before purchasing the animal.

- You should also understand the various other costs that you will encounter while raising your pet.

- These animals love playing and running around. These pets are fond of exploring things. They can create a mess if not monitored.

- If you are looking to earn money by harvesting and selling wool, then you should know that you will need to buy many rabbits for that. You will also have to invest a lot of money of their care you can earn from them.

Chapter 2: Owning a Mini Rex Rabbit

A pet is like a family member. You have to make sure that the animal is taken care of. The animal should be loved in your household. If your family is not welcoming enough for the pet, the animal will lose its sense of being very quickly.

You should be able to provide the pet a safe and sound home. Your family should be caring towards the pet. You have to be like a parent to the pet animal. This is the basic requirement when planning to bring an animal home.

If you wish to own a Mini Rex Rabbit or even if you already own one, it is important to understand the basic characteristics of the animal. You should know what you can expect from the animal and what you can't.

If the pet does not feel wanted and loved in your home, you will see a decline not just in its behaviour but also its health. This is the last thing that you should do to an animal. An animal deserves love and protection from the family members.

It should be noted that whether you keep a Mini Rex Rabbit for its invaluable wool or only as a friendly pet in the house, you will have to dedicate a lot of time to the animal. The animal will depend on you for its food and shelter needs. As the owner and the parent, it is your responsibility to make sure that you provide optimum conditions for the good well-being of your pet.

1. Getting home a healthy pet

There are many challenges that you will face while raising an animal at home. Your pet might face health issues that you would have to take care of. But, the last thing you want to do is to get an unhealthy animal home.

When you get an unhealthy or injured animal home, you make the road ahead more difficult. The animal could have health issues that might get worse with time. This only emphasises the fact that it is extremely important that you get a healthy Mini Rex Rabbit to your home.

Many a times, people get so excited about buying the animal that they forget to do the basic checks that need to be done before bringing the animal to your house. You should definitely do all the checks before you buy the Mini Rex Rabbit to avoid any future hassles.

It is always advised to discuss the health and also the history of the animal with the breeder before you buy the animal. A good breeder will not hesitate in sharing all the details about the animal with you.

You should make sure that you understand the various health issues that your future pet has suffered. If you are buying a Mini Rex Rabbit that is older in age then it is all the more important to make sure that you understand the history of the animal. Discuss in length about the various issues of the animal.

There are a few checks that you can conduct before you buy the Mini Rex Rabbit. The following checks will help you to make sure that your Mini Rex Rabbit is in good health and condition:

-   To begin with, check the coat of the animal. You should look for any abrasions on the Mini Rex Rabbit's skin. His skin should not be bruised from anywhere.

-   You should closely look for any injuries on the Mini Rex Rabbit. If you find some mark or injury, make sure that you understand the cause of the same. If it is a temporary issue, then it is fine. Discuss it with the breeder to make sure that the mark is not the indication of a serious issue with the Mini Rex Rabbit's health.

-   You should look for any hanging limbs in the animal. This is a clear indication of something being wrong with the animal. A hanging part of the body could mean that the pet is severely injured.

-   You should also check the animal's eyes. The eyes should not be dull. They should be bright and shiny. This can also be an indication to the animal's current health.

- The fur of the Mini Rex Rabbit is the index of its health. If the fur is soft and shiny, you can be sure that the animal is healthy. On the other hand, if the fur is not good, then the pet has health issues for sure.

- Another simple check that you can perform on your rabbit is to check the body temperature of the Mini Rex Rabbit. The body temperature should neither be too high or too low. Make sure you discuss the right temperature range of the rabbit with your breeder.

2. Licensing requirements

It is important to understand the licensing rules of the Mini Rex Rabbits. You should be sure that the laws permit you to hand raise the animal. This is important because the law prohibits the domestication of certain animals.

When you are planning to domesticate the Mini Rex Rabbits, you should understand the licensing laws properly. This would help you to avoid future hassles with the law.

Make sure that you understand all the laws that govern the domestication of the pet. You would definitely want to save yourself from any future trouble.

You should understand each detail before you go and buy the Mini Rex Rabbit. In case you domesticate an animal against the law, the penalty could even include seizure of the animal.

It is important that you understand that the steps of obtaining the license would essentially be the same in most places, there could be slight variations between the various regions.

Different regions would have their own regulation set. This makes it essential for you to contact the local council of your region. Different regions have will have their own rules.

United States licensing

If you are looking to domesticate a Mini Rex Rabbit in the United States of America, you need to understand the licensing rules in the country.

You don't need a license in United States to domesticate a Mini Rex Rabbit. Private breeders are to breed and sell rabbits for profits. You would require a licence if you would be using rabbits for research purposes.

If you wish to register your Mini Rex Rabbit, you will have to contact the rabbit clubs on your own. This will allow you to show your Mini Rex Rabbit.

It should be noted that all the dealers and breeders that make $600/£459.96 to $1000/£766.62 will have to get a USDA license. The commercial producers who sell the rabbits to pet stores should be licensed under the rules of AWA.

Each state has its own set of laws. Though the basic structure of the law that governs the keeping of these special animals is similar, the law will change as you move from one state to another.

It is advised that you consult the local municipal hall of your area to know the exact rules and regulations for domestication of the Mini Rex Rabbits.

United Kingdom licensing

The Rural land protection act of 1989 is the law of New South Wales that governs the domestication of Mini Rex Rabbits.

According to the law, anyone who wishes to domesticate more than two rabbits needs to have a license to do so. The law also makes it compulsory to vaccinate the rabbit with fibroma vaccine.

You can obtain a kit that will define all the conditions to domesticate the Mini Rex Rabbit can be obtained from the NSW office during office hours. The kit will also have the application form for a licence.

You can also expect an inspector to visit you and your rabbit to make sure that you adhere to all the rules. So, you should make sure that you fulfil all the criteria set by the law.

3. Things to know before you buy the Mini Rex Rabbit

When you decide to domesticate a Mini Rex Rabbit, there are many things that you should be looking. You should know where you can buy the animal from. You should also have the right information about various breeders in your state.

Selecting the right breeder

While you are all excited to buy your new pet animal, you should also make sure that you select the right breeder to buy the rabbit from. It is as important as buying the right pet. If you choose a wrong breeder, you will only have to face problems in the future.

It is important that you devote some time in looking for breeders in and around your region. It will pay to talk to other people who might have bought Mini Rex Rabbits in your region. They could help you in deciding the right breeders.

Finding the right breeder can be a challenging task, but it is a very important one. You can't be lax at this step. You should understand the reputation of the breeder before you choose him to buy your Mini Rex Rabbit.

There are some breeders who are into this profession for the love of Mini Rex Rabbits and animals in general. Of course they wish to earn money, but not by compromising their prime duty as a breeder.

On the other hand, you will also find breeders who do this only for the sake of money. Such breeders will not hesitate in providing you with the wrong information about the Mini Rex Rabbit such to make a few bucks. You need to save yourself from such selfish breeders. And, the best way to do this is by doing your homework right.

A good breeder will help you to know everything that you need to know about the animal that you intend to buy. He will not hide anything related to the health of the animal. As the potential buyer, you should know every little detail about your pet animal.

You need to make sure that the breeder you choose to buy the Mini Rex Rabbit from shares all the details about the rabbit. You should make sure that you understand the past of the rabbit and his health in great detail. This information will help you in the future to take care of your pet animal.

It is also important to understand here that a good breeder will also make sure that you can provide for the animal. He will ask you questions and will make sure that the animal will get a good owner and a good home. You can expect this from a breeder who cares enough for the animals that he keeps.

There have been cases where the breeders have denied permission to the prospective owners. This would be done considering the future of the Mini Rex Rabbit. A good breeder would always make sure that the animal goes into a safe environment. So if your breeder is asking you questions about how you intend to keep the animal, then this is a good sign.

The breeder would want to understand the prime motive behind your buying the Mini Rex Rabbit. Is it for the love of the animal or the wool? He would also want to understand if you have the time and energy to devote to the rabbit. The Mini Rex Rabbit can be demanding as a pet, and you should make sure that you can provide for him.

Keeping in mind the needs of the Mini Rex Rabbit, the breeder from whom you buy the rabbit will give you a set of instructions that will come in handy when you are taking care of the rabbit. You should make sure that you understand these instructions well.

List of rescue websites and breeders

It can be a very daunting task for a prospective owner to choose a breeder. You have to make sure that you choose the very best, so that you know that your pet has been in the right hands before you.

While you are choosing the breeder, you should also make sure that you understand the various breeds of the Mini Rex. You will have to make a decision to choose the breed that suits you the best. It is advised to understand these breeds well before you make a decision.

You might have many local pet shops in and around your place. These places could also sell Mini Rex Rabbits. You should buy the Mini Rex from the pet store if that is your only option. If you can buy the animal from a breeder, then it is better.

The problem with the pet stores is that you would not come to know about the history of the rabbit, which is so important to understand the health of the animal. You will also not be able to understand the breeding process and conditions of the animal. These are some important factors in determining the health and the history of the animal.

You have the option of adopting a Mini Rex Rabbit or buying it from a reputed breeder. There are some factors that will govern the final choice that you make. You should make sure that you understand these factors, so that you can make the right choice for yourself as the owner of a new pet.

If you are looking to bring an older Mini Rex to your home, then you should try to go for adoption. You can help a rabbit get a new home. Many rabbits are mistreated and abandoned by their owners. You can help to give one of these abandoned rabbits a new home. The abandoned Mini Rex Rabbit will get a new home and your family will get a new pet.

If you are looking at the financial side of the deal, then also you can benefit from adopting the rabbit. Many a times, you can expect to get a cage and other accessories with the abandoned rabbit. This will save you from building or buying a new cage for the animal.

Adopting the animal can serve to be a cheaper option for you than buying the same from the pet store or the breeder. On the other hand, if you are looking to hand raise a young rabbit then it is advised that you buy the same from a breeder.

Buying a young Mini Rex Rabbit from a breeder has its many benefits. You can talk to the breeder about the many concerns that you might have. You can understand the breeding procedure of the animal and can also be sure that the animal has been in safe hands before you.

If you are looking for an exhaustive list for the various reputed breeders, then the following list can help you:

- Rabbit haven: https://therabbithaven.org

- Rabbit breeders: http://rabbitbreeders.us

- Evergreen farm: www.evergreenfarm.biz

- Friends of rabbits: www.friendsofrabbits.org

4. Number of Mini Rex Rabbits you can keep

Just because you like an animal does not mean that you can keep tens of the same type together. Many a times, there are restrictions involved in keeping the same breed of animals together. It is important that you invest some time to understand these restrictions to avoid any future disappointments.

If you are planning to keep more than one Mini Rex Rabbit, you should understand their behaviour and space requirements. If you already have a Mini Rex Rabbit and are planning to buy more, you need to make sure that the pets can live harmoniously together.

When looking to domesticate more than one Mini Rex Rabbit, then one of the most important criteria that need to be kept in mind is the space that you would provide the rabbits. The animals need the right amount of space to grow and develop.

If you buy a new Mini Rex Rabbit and realize that he can't live harmoniously with the older one, what will you do? Will you just abandon him? This is not a very good idea. It is better to do your homework well before you make a decision.

These animals are known to be very active. You should be able to provide them a space where they can hop around without any constraints. There should be enough space for all the pets. If an animal has to compete with other animals for space, it will only lead to more trouble in the future.

You should understand that as the animals grow, they need more space. If you plan on keeping more than one rabbit, then you would have to give them more space when they grow. You should make sure that your house has the provision for the same.

The lesser the space for the animals, the more difficult it will get for you to raise your pets. So, space is one factor that will always be important when you are hand raising your pets. You should always keep this in mind.

The rabbits can get territorial and can fight with each other to establish their territory. You will have to keep a check on the pets to understand their basic behaviour and their urge to establish a territory.

There have been reported incidents where more than one Mini Rex Rabbit were able to live peacefully and happily in a cage. It will basically boil down to the individual temperaments of the animals. You will have to devote some time to understand the same.

The age of the Mini Rex Rabbits is another factor that should be taken into account by you. It is also known that if the Mini Rex Rabbits are introduced to each other at a very young age, there is a chance that they will get along well. The pets will grow together and will discover things together. This will help them to establish a bond amongst themselves.

It has been seen that pets usually get along with pets of their own age. A huge difference in age of rabbits can be a hindrance in their getting along with each other. So, if you are planning to domesticate more than one rabbit, make sure that they fall in the same age group.

No matter how things are looking, you should always keep a close eye on your pets. Never commit the mistake of leaving them on their own. You might not realize but they can harm each other. The first few interactions need to be all the more monitored.

Give the pets some time to know each other. Monitor their behaviour when they are away and when they are with each other. This will help you to understand how things are going. If you see things get out of hand, you should make sure that the pets are kept away from each other.

5. Mini Rex Rabbits and the other pets

The Mini Rex Rabbit is a social and loveable animal. You can expect your Mini Rex Rabbit to be friendly towards pets such as a pet dog or a pet cat. But this is not a rule, so you will have to make sure that the pets are comfortable with each other.

It is very important that each animal in the household is compatible with each other. If the animals are not getting along with one another then this would be mean that you can expect much chaos and trouble, not just for the animals but also for you and the other family members.

The type of pet is a very important criterion while determining whether the pets will get along or not. The Mini Rex Rabbit will definitely get along with another sociable and friendly pet. If it finds the other animal as a threat, then definitely they will not get along.

The age of the various pets is another factor that should be taken into account. It has been seen that pets usually get along with pets of their own age. A huge difference in age of pets can be a hindrance in their getting along with each other.

If your Mini Rex Rabbit is very young, you should make sure that you save him from bigger animals in the house. These animals might try to hurt the rabbit, and he would be too young to protect himself from any danger coming his way.

If you notice your pets not getting along well with each other, it is important that you don't force them to interact. They should be allowed to interact and bond in a very natural way. In the case where the pets can't get along even after multiple tries, you should keep them away from each other so that no one is harmed in any way.

6. Mini Rex Rabbits and children

There are many people who think that a rabbit is the perfect gift for a child in the house. But, before you blindly follow this advice and get your kid a Mini Rex Rabbit, you should make sure that you understand how well this will work in your home.

You should know that though Mini Rex Rabbits are cute and playful, they can also be very demanding. If you think that a child will be able to handle the pet on his own, then you might be wrong.

A Mini Rex Rabbit will need a lot of love and attention. A child's attention span will be short, and most probability he will not be able to provide the pet with the love and attention it needs. The Mini Rex Rabbit will feel unloved and this will affect his overall growth and development.

When the Mini Rex Rabbit is with the kid, it is important that all their interactions are supervised. This is to ensure the safety of the child and also the Mini Rex Rabbit. You should make sure that younger kids are not left alone with the pet so that they don't hurt themselves.

7. Taking care of the Mini Rex Rabbits

Mini Rex Rabbits will require lots of love and attention from your side. You will have to dedicate time for their grooming and also general care. You should also take out time to spend quality time with them.

If you are worried whether the bunny will be able to form emotional bonds in your home or not, then you shouldn't worry too much about it. If you focus on the right things and the rest will only follow.

You will be surprised to see how loyal and friendly your pet will be towards you. The pet will grow up to be friendly and affectionate. You can also form a good bond with the pet animal.

Like with other pets, once you form a personal bond with the bunny, it gets better and easier for you as the owner. If you get a young bunny home and spend your time and energy to raise him, you will notice as the animal grows older, it gets very fond of you.

The Mini Rex Rabbit is an animal that is known to have loads of energy. This will make him an active pet. You should lay emphasis on the quality of time you give to be with your bunny.

As the animal grows, he will value the bond that will be formed between the two of you. It is important that you make the right efforts for this bond to be formed between the bunny and you.

When you decide to domesticate an animal, it is more than important that you are prepared to solve the issues that might arise. You should be well equipped to do the same. Any animal will have certain requirements that you would have to fulfil if you wish to hand raise the animal.

The foremost concern of a prospective owner should always be to give the pet an environment that helps him to live happily. The pet should be able to grow and dwell in a healthy environment.

It is also important that you understand the licensing requirements of your area before you decide to domesticate the animal. This will help you avoid any legal hassles in the future regarding the domestication of the pet.

You should make all necessary arrangements to make sure that you provide the pet with all the necessities of food and shelter. This chapter will help you to understand the basic needs and requirements of your Mini Rex Rabbit. This will help you make all the necessary arrangements to domesticate the animal.

If you have other pets, such as cats and dogs in the house, then this could be a very important concern for you. If you are looking to get a new rabbit, then also the compatibility issues between the pet and the rabbit would be on the top of your mind.

It is important that the pets in the house get along with each other. This will make the atmosphere of the house very lively. You should look for the reactions that the pets have when they are with each other.

If the pets don't gel with each other, then it is not good for all the animals. As the owner, things will get difficult for you also because the primary concern of the owner is to give protection and safety to the pets.

You might have to keep them separate to make sure that everything in the house is fine. This is fine as long as they are not disturbing each other.

It is important that you understand the various criteria that will affect the compatibility of various pets with each other. These criteria will be of the temperament of the animals and also their age.

Sometimes, the animals don't intend to harm each other. But, they don't know how to behave with each other. In this confusion, they can end up harming each other.

So, as the owner you have to be on guard to make sure that all the animals are safe and no one is harmed.

8. Costs that you will incur

As a prospective owner, you might be wondering about the costs that you need to prepared for to domesticate the Mini Rex Rabbit. As the owner and parent of the pet, you will have to make attempts to fulfil all the needs of the animal. You should also be prepared on the financial front to take care of these needs.

It is better that you plan these things well in advance. This planning will help you to avoid any kind of disappointment that you might face when there are some payments that need to be made.

There are basically two kinds of costs that you will be looking to incur, which are as follows:

The one-time costs: The one-time costs are the ones that you will have to bear in the beginning when you decide hand raise a Mini Rex Rabbit. This will include the one-time payment that you will give to buy the animal.

There are other purchases that would come under this category, such as the permits and the license fee of the pet, purchasing price of food containers and the price of the enclosure.

The on-going costs: The on-going costs are the ones that you will have to spend each month or once in few months to raise the Mini Rex Rabbit. This category includes the costs of the food requirements and health requirements of the pet.

You should work out all these things right in the beginning, so that you don't suffer any problems later. Realizing at a later stage that you can't keep the animal and giving it up is never a good idea. You can maintain a journal to keep track of the costs.

Cost of Mini Rex Rabbit

The price of the Mini Rex Rabbit will depend on where you choose to buy the Mini Rex Rabbit from. You can get a rescued rabbit from a rescue centre or animal shelter, if it is available.

The next choice is to buy one from the breeder. The cost will vary depending on the quality of the Mini Rex Rabbit. A very good quality English Mini Rex Rabbit bought from a top class breeder will cost you around $175/£134.33.

Depending on your choice of breeder and the choice of Mini Rex Rabbit quality, you can expect to spend $50/£38.38 to $250/£191.90 for buying the bunny.

Health costs

It is important to include the cost of healthcare when working on various costs for the pet Mini Rex. This will help you to get an idea on what you can expect to spend on the general keep of the pet Mini Rex Rabbit.

The Mini Rex Rabbit does not require any shots or vaccinations, so you don't need to spend any money on the vaccinations.

The only regular medication that the Mini Rex needs is 'papaya enzyme tablets'. These tablets are required to keep the issue of wool block at bay. You can expect to spend about $10/£7.65 on 600 of these tablets.

These tablets don't need to be given daily. They can be given twice or thrice a week, so that means 600 tablets will last you a very long time.

You would be relieved to know that the Mini Rex Rabbit does not get sick that often. If you take care of the food and hygiene of the bunny, you can save him from many diseases. He will lead a healthy life if you take the necessary precautions.

You should always focus on the health of the Mini Rex Rabbit. This is necessary because an unhealthy animal is the breeding ground of many other diseases in the home. Your pet might pass on the diseases to other pets if not treated on time.

The rabbit will not fall sick that often, buy you should bring your pet to the veterinarian for regular check-ups. This is to avoid any future health problems.

You should also be prepared for unexpected costs, such as sudden illnesses or accidents of the Mini Rex Rabbit. Health care is provided at different prices in different areas. So, the veterinarian in your area could be costlier than the veterinarian in the nearby town.

Cost of food

A domesticated Mini Rex Rabbit will mostly be fed hay, grass and vegetables. You might also have to include various pellets and supplements to give your pet overall nourishment. It is important that you understand the food requirements of your Mini Rex in the beginning, so that you can be prepared on the monetary front.

You should feed about two cups of greens per day to the rabbit. This should cost you around $10/£7.68 per month. You can expect to pay $3/£2.32 to $5/£3.84 for the pellets.

You should make sure that there is enough fibre in the diet of the Mini Rex Rabbit. You need to feed timothy hay to the Mini Rex Rabbit every day. This should cost you about $3/£2.32 per month.

Cost of hygiene

A pet needs to be clean and hygienic. If you fail at maintaining hygiene levels for your pet, it will only lead to other complications. The basic hygiene of the pet can be maintained by a good quality shampoo and some towels.

There are many owners that insist on litter training. If you too wish to litter train your pet Mini Rex Rabbit, you will have to buy the required products for the same. You would need to buy paper litter for the bunny because it is safe even when the rabbit ingests it.

You will also be required to invest in a good detergent, which could be bleach. This will be needed to clean the cage and all the areas where the Mini Rex Rabbit might defecate.

This is a very basic amount that you will have to encounter. You should invest in some good cleaning products and sanitizers.

You can look at spending $4/£3.07 for the paper litter per month for the pet. The other requirements of shampoo and detergents should not cost you more than $10/£7.66 per month.

Cost of rabbit cage

The shelter of the animal will be his home, so it is important that you construct the shelter according to the animal's needs. If the pet is not indoors, it's most likely he will be in his cage. So, it is important to make this one time investment in a way that is best for the Mini Rex Rabbit.

The cage of the Mini Rex Rabbit should be six feet long, two feet wide and two feet wide. If you can provide extra space to the Mini Rex, it is better. The price of shelter will depend on the type of the shelter. You can expect to spend $20/£15.36 for the cage.

Miscellaneous costs

Although the main costs that you will encounter while raising your pet have already been discussed, but there will be some extra things that you will have to take care of. Most of these are one-time costs only.

You will have to spend money to buy stuff such as grooming comb, litter box, scissors, brush, nail clippers, feed bin, water bottle, accessories and toys for the pet. If you think that something needs to be repaired or replaced, you would have to spend money on doing that.

You can expect to spend some $100/£76.58 on these things. The exact amount will depend on the wear and tear and the quality of the products. In order to keep a track of things, you should regularly check the various items in the cage or hutch of the pet bunny.

9. Mini Rex Rabbit Vaccination

It is known that the Mini Rex Rabbits don't get sick very often. It is not necessary to give the bunnies shots or vaccines. But if you are in UK, then The Rural land protection act of 1989 makes it compulsory to vaccinate the rabbit with fibroma vaccine. The veterinarian might also advice the caregivers to give the Mini Rex Rabbits a vaccine against Calcivirus.

10. Mini Rex Rabbit Insurance

You can get insurance for your Mini Rex Rabbit. This insurance will help you to take care of the veterinarian bill and injury costs. Though the Mini Rex Rabbit does not get sick easily, a sudden procedure can cost you over thousands of pounds and dollars.

If you buy insurance to cover these conditions, you will save yourself from a lot of trouble. Depending on the insurance you buy, you can also cover regular clinic visits. There are some companies that will give you discounts on clinic visits.

There are some companies that can help you with Mini Rex Rabbit insurance, such as Exotic direct, pet plan and NCI. These companies have different kinds of insurance. You can choose according to your requirement. You can also get a package deal if you are looking to insure more than one Mini Rex Rabbits.

When you buy insurance, you have to pay a deductible amount and regular premiums. You will also be required to pay premiums that need to be paid regularly to keep the insurance policy active.

Rabbit insurance can cost you around $8/£6.14 to $20/£15.35 per month. The exact amount will depend on the company that you choose and also on the area where you live.

Chapter 3: Breeding in Mini Rex Rabbits

As a new or prospective owner of a Mini Rex Rabbit, you might be interested in the breeding cycle and procedure of the Mini Rex Rabbits. Breeding is defined as the process of production of an offspring by mating by the male and the female adults.

This chapter is meant to clear all your doubts regarding the breeding of Mini Rex Rabbits. It is important to understand the breeding patterns of your pet animals. How well you understand the mating patterns of your pet will also determine how well you look after the pet.

There are many owners who are interested in rabbits' breeding and production of the younger ones. The breeding at a controlled environment at your house can be challenging. But, it will get easier to understand once you equip yourself with all the right knowledge.

It is also known that the mother can sometimes kill the kits one after the other. There are many reasons behind this. The mother might do it when she is unable to provide nutrition to the kit.

If the kit has a danger of predators, such as wild dogs, even then the mother might decide to kill the kits. It is important that the mother rabbit is kept under observation during her nesting phase.

If your female rabbit tends to kill its young one, you will have to keep the little ones away from her. It is known that if the mother kills more than two of her kits, she should not be allowed to breed again.

1. Mating behaviour of the Mini Rex Rabbits

You should understand the natural mating behaviour of your Mini Rex. This will help you to do the right thing while breeding them. This chapter is meant to equip you with all the knowledge that you might need while mating your rabbits.

Each animal species have their unique breeding habits and patterns. When you are looking to take care of your pet well, you should also lay enough emphasis on understanding its breeding patterns.

The male Mini Rex Rabbit gets sexually mature at the age of seven to eight months, while the female Mini Rex Rabbits get sexually mature a month earlier, which is six to seven months of age.

It should also be noted that the different breeds of Mini Rex differ slightly in the time by which the males and females reach sexual maturity.

The younger Mini Rex Rabbits are referred to as bunnies or kits. A male and female Mini Rex are able to produce many kits at a single time. These rabbits are known to be very active sexually. Anyone looking to breed rabbits and produce kits will not be disappointed.

It should be understood that rabbits are able to follow one mating cycle with the other in short durations of time. This means that if the mating procedure of the Mini Rex Rabbits is not understood and controlled, your house could be flooded with kits.

A good breeder will always encourage you to thoroughly understand the sexual tendencies of your rabbits, so as to not commit any mistake in the future. You need to know how often and in what conditions your rabbits can reproduce.

In the wild, the kits have higher chances of survival in a warm environment. This means that the rabbits enter their mating cycle in warmer temperatures. You can expect the same when the rabbits are domesticated.

When a rabbit is in its natural environment, the extra amount of light during the summers and also spring brings about a change in its body. The male and female rabbits get sexually active during this time.

A male rabbit will display changes in its behaviour. It will seem more aggressive and restless. This is due to the sex hormones that have become active in its body. This is how you can identify if your male Mini Rex is ready to mate or not.

Another interesting behaviour that can be noted in the males is that they become more competitive with other male rabbits. The males who are sexually active compete with each other to establish dominance in the group. This is done so that they can impress the female and attract her for mating.

It is known that in the wild, the dominant male Mini Rex has a good sex life in comparison to the shy ones. When you see your pet male Mini Rex getting too aggressive and competitive, you should know that he is ready for mating.

When your male rabbit and female rabbit are ready for mating, you should bring the female rabbit to the male rabbit's cage. It should be noted that the opposite should not be done.

You should not take the male rabbit to the female rabbit's cage because the female rabbit can get territorial. You might find the female attacking and harming the male instead of mating with him.

Once the male rabbit (buck) is able to attract the female rabbit (doe), the mating can begin. During the process, the female will lie down on a level surface on the ground as an invitation to the male rabbit. The female will also lift its tail.

The male will mount himself on the female rabbit at this time. The male is known to cast a sharp bite on the nape of the female at this time. This process should last over twenty seconds.

The mating process will end here and the male will release the female at this time. It should also be noted that the male rabbit will have fur in his mouth because of the bite he had cast. He will also lose consciousness for some time after the entire process is over.

Now, the female is pregnant. The gestation period in the female will last for over a month. Once that is over, you can expect your pregnant Mini Rex to give birth to three to eight kits or bunnies.

It should be noted that the new born kits are hairless. They are also blind at this time. The female is capable of repeating the same process and giving birth to bunnies many times in a year.

2. Nesting

When you are conducting controlled mating at your home, then there are many things that you will have to take care of. You should make sure that the male and the female rabbit are in the same cage when they both are ready.

After they have mated, you should be ready to take care of the doe. It is also important that you take care of the nesting requirements of the rabbits once the mating is over and the female rabbit is pregnant.

The nesting box is a box that will be used by the female rabbit as the nest. She will give birth to the bunnies in the nest. You should make sure that the box is big enough to allow the rabbit to be comfortable. The young ones will spend a lot of time in the nesting box, so it should be as comfortable as possible.

You should only place the nesting box in the rabbit cage when the time is right. If you keep it in any earlier, the rabbit will try to dig it as if it is digging a burrow. The rabbit might also use the box as litter box. Make sure that this does not happen.

The kits are expected after one month of the female getting pregnant. So, you should ideally keep the nesting box in the cage of the rabbit on the twenty eighth day after mating has taken place.

The female is expected to give birth anytime from the twenty eighth day to the thirty first day after mating. Of course, the mating should have been successful.

You should put some soft pine and hay in the nest box before keeping it in the cage of the rabbit. This will give a cushion like structure to the nest. It will make the nest box cosy and comfortable.

There is a natural tendency of the female rabbit that is about give birth. She will pull out some hair from under her chin. This will be used by her as a cushion for the young ones that are to arrive.

The doe will use this nesting box to give birth to the young ones. Initially, the young ones will spend all their time in the box. This is because they will be too small to come out of the nesting box.

After the female rabbit gives birth to the bunnies in the nest, she will try to spend most of the time outside the nest. You will see her in the cage, but outside the nest box. The mother will get into the cage to feed the young ones. You can expect this to happen at least twice a day.

After three weeks, you will see that the young ones have started coming out of the nest. They will keep hopping in and out of the nest box at this time.

When you notice that the bunnies are spending a good amount of time outside the box, you should remove the box. The kits don't need it anymore.

3. Raising a baby rabbit

When you get a pet home, it is more like a new member in the family. It is very important that you take time to understand the various stages in the pet's life. Each stage will demand for different care and methods.

In case you decide to breed your Mini Rex Rabbit, you will face the situation where you will have to take care of a kit. There are many people who buy kits from the breeders. They also have to face the same situation.

Hand rearing a baby rabbit can be very tricky, but if you pay attention to the details, it will be fun and interesting. You should take care of a few things to make sure that your baby rabbit is taken care of.

When a baby rabbit or kit is born, he has no hair. He is also blind and deaf. You shouldn't be surprised to see this condition. You can expect the kit to get his first hairs after a few days of his birth.

The kit will open his eyes after approximately ten days. This is the time when the ears of the kit also start to open.

It should also be noted that body temperature regulation is very important for a Mini Rex Rabbit. But, a baby rabbit is unable to regulate the temperature of his body. It is only after 7-8 days that you can expect him to do so.

Breeding in Mini Rex Rabbits can happen after the doe gives birth to the babies. People who breed rabbits for wool generally wait for 40-42 days before they rebreed.

The female rabbit will give birth to about twelve kits at a time. Some can even give birth to larger number of kits than twelve. A female rabbit will have about eight to ten nipples. This makes it easier for her to feed all her kits.

If due to some reason, a mother is not capable of taking care of the young one, then the kits can be given to another female rabbit that is in the same age group as the mother. This should be done in the first few days of kindling, preferably first three days.

The kits are weaned after about five weeks of their birth. Even when they are feeding off the mother, they need to do it twice a day. Each feed time will last for about three to four minutes.

You need to be well prepared when you have to hand rear an infant. It can be very challenging if you don't get your basics right. You should make sure that you do the right things for the kit.

While you might have learnt it all, there are a few important points that need to be remembered taking care of the infant Mini Rex Rabbit. You will have to be patient with your pet infant. This is the key.

Try to understand the position of a new born and never force him to do anything. Just try to give him a warm and secure environment. This is very important.

If you are hand raising the infant rabbit, then you need to substitute the mother rabbit's milk. This can be easily done.

When you feed the milk formula to the baby rabbit, you should make sure that the milk is at the temperature of the blood of the infant. This is a very important point. There is a simple formula for the feed that you should be giving your infant bunny.

Take half cup of water, half a cup of evaporated milk, one tsp. of corn starch and one egg yolk and mix everything together. One tablespoon of this formula should be given once or twice in a day.

The kits will start eating green leaves and grass after fifteen to twenty days of their birth. You can introduce the greens to them at this time along with the milk formula. This will take care of their daily nutritional requirement.

It is important to note that the infant of the rabbit has absolutely no way of keeping itself warm for the first week after its birth. It can't regulate its temperature, yet it should be kept warm to keep it safe.

You will have to make sure that the baby rabbit is experiencing the right temperatures. He has to be warm at all times. But, make sure that the temperature does not get too hot. This can also be harmful for the rabbit.

Before you can start feeding your kit, wrap the infant safely in a blanket. This will help to keep the infant warm. You will have to constantly monitor the temperature so that it does not over heat the infant.

You should keep the infant close to you as much as possible. Your body warmth is also important for the infant to feel safe. When you are feeding him with the bottle, try to keep the blanket or pouch carrying him close to your body in your lap.

You can try opening the mouth of the infant with the help of your index finger and thumb. Make sure that you are as gentle and soft as possible.

You can also close his eyes with your hand when you are trying to feed him. These are simple tricks that can help you to feed a baby that is not being very cooperative.

It might take some time, but the infant rabbit will become a little settled with time. You will see him being more comfortable and less restless. You should be a little patient and kind with the rabbit.

Another important point that you need to know is that the bottle being used to feed the baby rabbit should never be squeezed when the nipples are in the baby's mouth. The infant is still learning. The infant's body is still developing.

When you squeeze the bottle, there could be a rush of milk inside the infant's body. The liquid could even enter the baby's lungs. So, the best way is to let the animal drink at his pace.

The initial phase of trying to nurse the infant can be stressful and challenging for you. But slowly as the days will progress, things will get easier. It has been noticed with the infant rabbits that they might take some time to get used to you and the new surroundings.

But, once the infant get used to you and the environment, you will have a great emotional bond with them. The nursing time will also become easier and also memorable.

If your infant is rejecting the milk or the milk formula that is being served to him, then there could be another reason than him being uncomfortable in the new surroundings. It is possible that the animal is rejecting it because he feels unsafe.

You should make sure that the water you use to prepare the formula has been cooled after heating it. It should be noted that you should not use cold water because it is not right for the formula.

You should also not water that isn't boiling because it can again destroy the mineral content of the formula. A simple way to make use of the water is to boil the water, and then let the boiled water cool down.

When you try to feed the baby rabbit, he might resist the feed or might just reject it completely. This is a normal behaviour by the kit and you should patiently keep trying. Don't force him. Just gently keep trying and finally the kit will take to the milk formula and also the feeding method.

It is known that the young ones can be affected by bowel related diseases and the diseases that directly affect the urinary tract. It will be difficult to control the infection once it starts spreading. The joey is too young to have any immunity against such diseases.

It is important that you look for the first signs of infection. If you see something is wrong, you should make sure that you consult the vet as soon as possible.

While you are feeding the baby rabbit, you should be very particular about the hygiene of the baby and his surroundings. If there is any milk spillage, clean it immediately so that the area does not become a breeding place for diseases and infections.

In most cases of Mini Rex Rabbit domestication, people buy kits from a breeder. It becomes essential to understand the baby bunny and give him an environment that closely resembles to what it would have been if he was with to his mother.

There is also a probability that you have rescued the infant from the wild. If you have rescued a litter, then it becomes all the more that difficult for you. This is because the infant must be scared and you will have to work on him on an emotional level.

The baby rabbit could be trapped or could be in danger of predators. You will have to take into account the condition of the infant when you are making a plan of how to care for your bunny.

You should understand the baby Mini Rex Rabbit would be very sacred of all the new things coming its way. You have to be well prepared for this.

Be kind and have some empathy towards the bunny. Even if it is difficult for you to see the scared kit, you need to be calm. The kit will get better with time and with the care you provide it.

Mini Rex Rabbits can grow up to be very good pets if they are loved and cared for in the beginning. This first year is a crucial time because this is when the kit forms intimate bonds with human beings.

The emotional bonds that it forms at this stage will stay with him for his life. He will be loyal towards them. Make sure that you pay as much attention to the development of the infant rabbit.

When the Mini Rex Rabbit is very young, it is always advised to keep him under constant observation. He should be supervised by you at all times. Even if you are not around and are busy, then a family member should be around the rabbit.

You should also be careful when you are planning to start solid foods for the baby rabbit. Even though the baby rabbit is ready, you can't start giving him the adult food right away.

As the owner of a Mini Rex Rabbit, you might be surrounded by many questions. It is important that you learn about the right time and the right ways to introduce solid food to the little one. The kit will enjoy its food as much as it enjoyed its milk.

You should start with introduction of simpler solid foods in the baby Mini Rex Rabbit's diet. This will help him to develop his digestive tract before he can start eating the real adult food of the Mini Rex Rabbits.

Chapter 4: Habitat of the Mini Rex Rabbit

By now, you would have made a decision whether you want to domesticate a Mini Rex Rabbit or not. It should be noted that whether you keep a Mini Rex Rabbit for its invaluable wool or only as a friendly pet in the house, you will have to dedicate a lot of time to the animal.

The animal will depend on you for its food and shelter needs. He can't tell you what he needs. As the owner and the parent, it is your responsibility to make sure that you provide optimum conditions for the good well-being of your pet.

The Mini Rex will need a lot of love and care from your side. If you are sure that you have the time and the energy to care for the pet, then you will have a great time with your pet. One of the main concerns that you should have while you are planning to hand raise the animal is that you need to provide good shelter for the pet.

It is very important that you understand the habitat requirements of your pet. But before you can do so for your pet, you should be able to understand what your Mini Rex Rabbit needs. Do your homework right and understand his requirements.

This chapter will help you in doing just the same. By the end of it, you will be able to understand what the right habitat conditions are for your Mini Rex Rabbit.

If you can't provide your pet a habitat that keeps him happy and safe, then you will fail as the parent of the pet. You need to make sure that the pet gets what would make it happy and comfortable. The animal can slip into sadness and depression if his habitat requirements are not met.

This might seem quite new to you. When you think of it, you will realize the importance of a habitat in an animal's life. Imagine being uprooted from your home and being kept in conditions that don't suit your natural ways of living? Wouldn't that create misery in your life?

You should make sure that you have the provision to keep the animal indoors when required. Also, thorough understanding of its living conditions in the natural habitat is necessary so that you can provide him an environment that best suit its requirements and needs.

Every animal is so used to its own natural surroundings that as the owner of a new Mini Rex Rabbit, you should make sure that you fulfil the habitat requirements of your pet animal. A comfortable home would hopefully mean a happy pet.

1. Understanding the pet's requirements

A Mini Rex Rabbit is a very intelligent and smart animal. You can easily train him to suit your family and living conditions. The rabbit will get accustomed and used to the family very easily and pretty soon.

Because the animal is easy to keep and train you can keep the rabbit indoors most of the time. The furry little animal will soon become a part of your family. This is also good for the well-being of the Mini Rex Rabbit.

While you should keep the pet indoors most of the time, it is also important that there is a provision for a cage for the animal. This cage will be useful when the pet needs to be kept isolated. When the pet is sick, he might need the space to recuperate and get better.

If the Mini Rex Rabbit is not under supervision, he can get very mischievous. The animal will chew at things, even electrical wiring. This can pose a danger to him and also others. So, either you should supervise the rabbit or keep him in a place where he does not need supervision and is safe.

When you or any other family member is not around, the cage will be very useful at such times. You can be sure that the rabbit is safe and sound while you are busy at your work. This makes it important that you have the provisions for a cage for the animal.

The pet should be used to being in the cage for some part of the day, so that it is easier for him when he has to stay in it. So, make sure that you keep the animal in cage sometimes. You should understand that the cage would also serve as the resting spot for the pet. The enclosure will keep it safe and will also protect him from various outside dangers.

It is only critical that the enclosure is designed in a way so that maximum comfort, protections and security is guaranteed to the rabbit. This chapter will help you to understand how you can build the ideal enclosure for your pet Mini Rex Rabbit.

When you bring the Mini Rex Rabbit to your home, you should spend as much time as possible with him. During this time, you should keep it indoors. It is necessary that the rabbit spends as much time as possible with you.

You should treat the animal as a part of your family. Shower love and affection on him and help him to get used to the new surroundings. This is the time when you will form a bond with your pet.

It should also be noted that as your pet grows and matures, it needs some extra physical space for itself. It will need the space to grow, play and hop around. In their natural habitat, the rabbits are used to a lot of space.

The rabbits are used to jumping around and hopping around. This is a natural tendency for them and also a part of their personality. You can't confine them to a corner of the house. So, you should be able to give them the desired space even in your home.

The enclosure also needs to be escape proof. No matter how comfortable the pet is with you; there are some precautions that you will have to take. What if your Mini Rex Rabbit decides to just escape from a gap in the enclosure?

Make sure the enclosure is designed and built keeping in mind this particular point. Even if the rabbit escapes accidentally, you will not be able to find him. To avoid the trouble for you and the poor pet, you should design a safe and escape proof cage.

The habitat should be kept as real and natural as possible. You can't create a habitat for a fish when you are domesticating a rabbit. There are specific needs for each animal, even for their habitats. It is important that you understand the habitat requirements of the Mini Rex Rabbit.

The pet animal should feel comfortable and easy in the enclosure. This is the basic requirement of the habitat. The structure and furnishing should resemble his natural habitat. This will make the animal as if it is in its natural home.

The enclosure should be built in a way that is predator proof. The enclosure should be able to provide the necessary protection and safety. The rabbit would not be able to protect itself in case of any danger. As the prospective owner, you need to provide for this requirement.

You should make an in-depth analysis of the various predators that could attack the pet animal in his enclosure. You should plan the safety measures keeping in mind the strength of the predators.

You should also focus on the emotional health of the animal. The enclosure should make the pet emotionally safe. He needs to feel safe and secure in the setting. He needs to be comfortable and happy.

If you are unable to provide a comfortable home for the Mini Rex Rabbit, he will get stressed and worked up. This will show in his health and behaviour also. So, you should make sure that the enclosure should give him the space to de-stress and relax.

The enclosure you build will depend on the space that you can afford to have. Though the rabbit is very small and does not require much space, he needs space to walk around and play. The rabbits are very active and thus more space is always a blessing for them.

As an owner, it is important for you to understand the temperament of your pet Mini Rex Rabbit. The Mini Rex Rabbit can't be kept captive for too long. This puts a negative effect on him. Even if the cage is very comfortable, make sure you bring him out of the same.

He should be allowed to release his energy by running around. This pent up energy can make him very negative and ferocious. The Mini Rex Rabbit will turn sad and will only become dull with each passing day.

If you have a big house and an extra room in that house, then you can also designate one room for the pet Mini Rex Rabbit. The room will be like the home of the pet. He can sleep, play, eat or do whatever he wants to do in there. If you are keeping one room for the Mini Rex Rabbit, then you should furnish it with the right things.

The rooms should be spacious and airy. There should be a lot of toys in the room for the Mini Rex Rabbit to play. If you are looking at buying some toys for the Mini Rex Rabbit, then you can choose from toys that are durable and also the ones that can't be shredded.

All these toys and fun items will be a source of great amusement and fun for the Mini Rex Rabbits. It is also important that you bunny proof this particular room.

2. Keeping the Mini Rex Rabbit indoors

There are many people who prefer to keep the Mini Rex Rabbits indoors. This is actually the best environment for the pet. But, a lot will depend on your household and your living conditions. You should make a note of this before you take a decision.

You should also know that it won't be easy. The pet can be very challenging at times. So, you have to be prepared for the challenges that come along. This will also help you make a decision on whether you really want a bunny, if you still don't have one.

While you might be okay with the idea of your Mini Rex Rabbit staying indoors most of the times, but you should also make sure that all of the other family members are also fine with this decision. If the family is comfortable with the pet, it is only then that the pet will feel the love and warmth.

Like many other pets, the Mini Rex needs to be supervised at all times. If you don't supervise him, he will destroy things in a bid to explore stuff. To make things easier for you, you should build a cage for the pet.

You should have a provision for a cage inside the house, so that you can put the Mini Rex in the cage when no one is around to supervise him. This is a simple way to keep the pet around and also be sure that he is not destroying stuff.

In the wild, the Mini Rex Rabbit will live under boulders and rocks. He will jump and hop around. You should know that the rabbits can dig very deep tunnels and burrows. They might even spend most of their time there. These places are safe grounds for resting and taking care of the young ones.

The natural characteristics of an animal will always come into play even when it is domesticated. They will always go back to their natural mannerisms and way of being. This understanding will help you to understand your pet animal better.

The Mini Rex Rabbit has the agility and strength to dig for a very long time. When you domesticate a Mini Rex Rabbit, you might find your Mini Rex Rabbit finding comfort under a chair or other piece of furniture. You will also see them to dig tunnels and holes in sand and gardens.

You can always take the decision to keep the pet indoor. In fact, the Mini Rex Rabbit will be very happy and secure indoors. The pet will feel safe and you will also be able to monitor what the pet is up to.

You can also keep a cage for the pet. But, there is no need to keep him in the cage if you will be around. You can use the cage when you are sleeping or are busy with something else. This will allow you to be free.

3. Building the ideal cage for the Mini Rex Rabbit

It is very important to design and build the right enclosure for the Mini Rex Rabbit. The enclosure will be like a home to the Mini Rex Rabbit, so it is very important that the enclosure meets all the requirements of the Mini Rex Rabbit.

The habitat should be spacious, comfortable and safe for the pet. The pet should feel at home in the habitat that you provide it. You should try to furnish the enclosure in a way that the cage resembles the natural habitat of the Mini Rex Rabbit. This will keep him happy and upbeat, which is essential for his overall well-being.

A good amount of enclosure space is essential when designing and planning the cage. This is because the pet rabbit needs some space to move around. The cage should not feel like a prison. It has to be safe and secure.

Getting the right measurements and dimensions for the enclosure is an important part of designing the cage. This will help you to plan the outer periphery and the area of the enclosure. So, it is important to plan it well and construct it with the right technique.

The ideal cage of the rabbit should be six feet long, two feet tall and two feet wide. These dimensions of the enclosure are the minimum requirements of the Mini Rex Rabbit.

This is a must and you should make sure to provide the animal with such a habitat. It is always better to give the rabbit or rabbits a more spacious environment. If you are planning to get more pets, then you need more space.

There might be an instance when you would have to isolate your Mini Rex Rabbit. Your habitat should allow you to do so. The isolation could be needed due to some disease or infection that the animal could be suffering from.

The isolated area would help the animal to be treated well. He will be able to heal and get better. He will also get the much needed isolation. This will also help in keeping the other pets in the house safe.

A simple trick that you can use to make the animal comfortable with the cage is to instruct the bunny to go inside the cage, but leave the door of the cage open. If you do this, the Mini Rex Rabbit will also not feel captive. Let the Mini Rex come out and go inside the cage at will, but make sure that it spends considerable time in the cage.

It is important the pet is not forced to go into the cage. He should find the cage homely and should go there without a hesitation. This exercise should only be done under your supervision. This will allow him to get acquainted with the cage.

If you are unable to supervise the pet for some reason, then don't make the mistake of keeping the cage door open. You should keep the cage door closed so that the pet stays inside. This is to avoid any unpleasant incidents.

You should always remember that no matter how much you train the Mini Rex Rabbit, you can be surprised and shocked by him. He is a playful, chirpy and hyperactive animal and will not leave any chance to do some mischief.

It is extremely important that you clean the cage regularly. A dirty cage will only lead to infections for the pet and also the other pets. You should clean the cage daily and should change the food and water provided for him.

The outdoor enclosure should be planned and constructed keeping in mind the basic nature of the Mini Rex Rabbit. The animal should have fun, but should also be safe and should not get any opportunity to run away from the enclosure.

The enclosure needs to be constructed with high quality material. The outer area of your garden and backyard should also be covered. You can look at using the chain links that are utilized to build cyclone fences. These fences are very strong and durable.

There is a chance that while playing, the Mini Rex Rabbit's head might just get stuck in the gap in the fence. To prevent any such accident, you can install a preventive wire outside the main fence. This will ensure that the Mini Rex Rabbit does not get trapped when you are not around.

A Mini Rex Rabbit is a good climber. You have to make preventive measures so that the Mini Rex Rabbit does not climb out. You should make sure that the enclosure has fencing on the top area. The Mini Rex Rabbit also loves digging.

It should also be taken care of that the Mini Rex Rabbit can't dig and eventually escape the enclosure. The enclosure should be safe and also well fenced. This will make sure that the Mini Rex Rabbit can't escape.

To make things look like his natural habitat, cover the floor with sand, plants, wooden chips and twigs. Your house should have fencing to protect the pet animal from stray animals. The pet should be able to be at peace when in the enclosure. He should be able to do whatever he wants to do.

4. Rabbit hutch

Building a rabbit hutch is one of the most popular choices of the owners of the Mini Rex Rabbits. You should make sure that you have the provision to build the same in your house. You can keep one in the backyard, basement or any other area of the house.

A rabbit hutch can be defined as a cage for the rabbit that is constructed generally with wood and a wire mesh that surrounds it. Most rabbit hutches have long legs to keep them anywhere. The ones without legs can be placed over tables or other safe surfaces.

It is important that you understand that the rabbit hutch is only one option that you have when your pet needs to be kept in a cage-like environment. This does not mean that you can keep the pet in the hutch and forget about him comfortably.

The hutch needs to be easily accessible to the family members. You should keep a check on the rabbit from time to time. You should also allow the pet some time outside the hutch to just walk around.

Many cases have been reported in the past where the owners' negligence towards the Mini Rex Rabbits caused serious issues in the animals. You can't abandon your rabbit in a comfortable hutch. The pet should be kept indoors as much as possible. The hutch can be used when you are not around to care for the pet.

You can buy the rabbit hutch or can design it yourself. It is important that it meets all the requirements of the pet animal. To begin with, the hutch needs to be spacious. The animal should have enough space to walk around.

You should make sure that the rabbit hutch does not suffocate the rabbit. It should be airy and well ventilated. You should make sure that the rabbit has access to food and water in the rabbit hutch. You can install a feed hopper and a good watering system in the rabbit hutch to ensure the same.

You should also try to make the hutch attractive for the rabbit. He should not feel bored and suffocated in there. The hutch should feel like a fun home for him. There are some simple ways in which you can make the hutch a lively place for the rabbit.

Keep some small and interesting toys for the Mini Rex Rabbit in the hutch. You should make sure that the toys don't scare the pet away. They should be inviting and fun for him. This will keep him happy and entertained.

The rabbit hutch should allow proper sanitation. Many cases of diseases have been reported in Mini Rex Rabbits due to improper sanitation. If you wish to see your pet healthy, you need to make sure that the hutch provides proper sanitation for the same.

The rabbit's hutch would need to be cleaned regularly to make sure that there are no disease carrying bacteria and virus in there. These are simple things, but critical when it comes to the well-being of the pet in the long run.

The nest boxes that are used for the kits should be sanitized regularly. They should be stored safely and properly when not in use. You can store them and use them for the next set of kits that you might have.

The food and water systems should also be regularly cleaned. This is very important because if you fail to do so, the rabbit will always be at a risk of some life threatening disease. To avoid such a scenario, sanitize regularly.

If you are planning to keep more than one Mini Rex Rabbit, then you can work on giving them a common habitat. Some people would choose to give separate shelters to the animals. The idea of providing separate shelters is also fine.

If the pets get along, then they can be kept in a common cage. But, in case the rabbits are not getting along then keeping them in a common cage will only lead to more problems in the future, so this should be avoided.

5. Furnishing the enclosure

You could also furnish the enclosure of your pet. The furnishings will make the animal more comfortable and the enclosure more beautiful. There are several ways in which you can furnish the enclosure that you have constructed.

The furnishing should also be designed keeping in mind the comfort and also the security of the pet. The furnishing should not in any way disturb the lifestyle of the rabbit. It should gel with the personality of the animal.

It is important that you understand the significance of accessorising the cage of the pet animal. The accessories should add on to the living experience of the animal. They should definitely not be a barrier of any kind for the Mini Rex Rabbit.

Furnishing the enclosure makes the enclosure more comfortable and appealing. The animal should like the furnishing. Look out for any signs that your pet does not like the furnishing. Anything that the animal is not comfortable with should be removed.

Accessorising the cage will give a good feel to the cage. The cage will seem more like a home and less like a prison to the Mini Rex. You should always look for things that the animal would find in his natural habitat.

You can look at items such as leafy branches, small logs and shrubs as accessories in the cage. The idea behind the leafy branches and logs is to give the pet an environment that closely resembles this natural habitat. This will keep him happy and spirited.

You can also keep toys for your Mini Rex Rabbits. These toys will keep him happy and entertained. The right kind of toys should be bought for the pet. You will get many ideas when you visit a shop that sells toys for rabbits.

It is better if the toys are washable. This will enable you to wash the toys every now and then when they are dirty. The harmful bacteria will also be removed from the toys when they are washed. This is important to maintain good health of the Mini Rex Rabbit.

There are many kinds of toys that you can buy for your pet animal. But, it is important that the toys are made of a good quality material. They should not be harmful for the pet. Your Mini Rex Rabbit will take them in his mouth, so they should be of a good quality.

Also, make sure that the toys are durable and non-toxic. If the pet is able to shred the toy, he will swallow the shreds. This is very harmful and will only invite more trouble for the pet. To avoid all these issues, invest your money to buy the right kind of toys.

You can also keep a couple of warm blankets inside the cage. There should be a lot of toys in the cage for the Mini Rex to play with. The bunny will play and will also bite these toys. The rabbit will like snuggling the blanket. You should try to make the cage as comfortable as possible, so that the pet animal does not feel like a captive and starts liking the cage.

6. Cleaning the enclosure

Proper sanitation is extremely important to keep the pet rabbit healthy. If you don't give time to sanitation, you will only make things difficult for the Mini Rex pet.

There are certain tasks that you need to do daily, while several others need to be done once a week. Similarly, if the food and water containers look dirty, they should be cleaned and refilled. The litter box needs to be cleared every day.

The pet can't clean the cage on its own, and if it is forced to stay in an unhygienic environment, he will fall sick. It is extremely important to clean the cage of the pet. You will not necessarily enjoy this process, but still you have to do it.

Once a week, you should clean the entire cage. You should thoroughly clean it with a clean cloth. Remember that the pet should not be in the cage when the cleaning procedure is going on. The litter box needs to be disinfected once a week. The toys of the pet should be washed once every two weeks, if the toys are washable.

It is important that the cage is free from all bacteria and viruses that are known to cause diseases in pet animals. You should keep some time designated for the cleaning of the cage.

Another point that you need to understand is that you should not use very strong disinfectants. Such products can be very harmful if they are ingested even in the smallest of quantities. You should always look for mild anti-bacterial soaps and detergents to clean the vessels and the floor.

A simple procedure that you can follow once every week to clean the cage thoroughly is to fill a bucket with clean water. Pour some anti-bacterial detergent that you wish to use. Form a nice lather in the bucket. This can be used to clean the toys and the containers. The remaining can be used to clean the floor nicely.

After you have cleaned the floor with the detergent, use plain water to wash off any sign of the detergent. This will ensure that the pet does not ingest anything harmful. It is also very important that you let the floor dry completely before you allow the Mini Rex Rabbit to come inside the cage.

He could spoil the floor and could create a mess for you to clean again. He could even try to drink any residue that he finds on the floor. To avoid all these hassles, you should allow the floor to dry completely.

Chapter 5: Bunny proofing the house

Your Mini Rex Rabbit is a cute and small animal, but if proper precautions are not taken, it can create havoc in your home. It is very important that you learn the simple ways to bunny proof the home.

The worst nightmare of any prospective caregiver is when the pet animal creates a mess in the house. This can be very difficult for anyone that wishes to domesticate an animal.

Though bunnies are very calm by their natural demeanour, they are also very curious. They have the capacity to chew off things if they are not supervised from time to time.

When you have a pet at home, you have to ensure that the pet is safe at all times. This is one of your basic responsibilities as the pet owner. A rabbit has a very curious personality.

The Mini Rex Rabbit will not think twice before charging into unknown territory. The animal is so small that he can easily get himself into problems. This makes it very important that you understand the behaviour of your pet very well.

This chapter is meant to help you to understand the various ways to bunny proof your home. Make sure you bunny proof your home and keep your pet bunny away from potential dangers.

You might be busy with some work, and before you know your pet Mini Rex might be walking into some real danger. It is important to learn some basic ways to bunny proof the house.

When you take appropriate measures to bunny proof the house, you can actually go a long way in ensuring that the rabbit is safe and there are no unwanted incidents in the house.

It is always better to take precautions, rather than lamenting when major damage has been done because in most cases, the damage can't be reserved or undone.

You should know that your per bunny has a tendency to injure himself. If you don't pay attention, the damage could be very serious and irrevocable. A very simple solution to keep your pet animal safe is to bunny proof your home.

This chapter will discuss the potential dangers to the Mini Rex Rabbits and also some simple ways to bunny proof your house. They will help you to avoid mishaps and also keep the Mini Rex Rabbit safe at all times.

1. Why should you bunny proof your house?

Many of you might be wondering why it is so important to bunny proof the house. If you fail to bunny proof your house, you might find your pet seriously injuring himself.

It is important that you take appropriate steps to bunny proof the home. This will help you to set some limits and boundaries for the pet. These boundaries are for his own good.

There is no use in getting cautious after serious and irrevocable damage has been done. It pays to take all the necessary precautions right from the very beginning.

You will take some time to understand the mannerisms of your pet. It is important to always supervise the pet. But, once you understand the pet better, you can take steps to make sure that things remain safe in the house for the pet. A safe environment is good for everybody in the home.

If you are unable to do so, you can ask a family member to do so for you. You can use the cage when there is no one around to supervise the pet rabbit. You can be secure knowing that your pet is safe and sound inside its cage.

The rabbit can injure himself and can also lead to mishaps in the house. This can be very dangerous not just for the rabbit, but also for the family members.

You should be very serious about pet proofing your home. Your Mini Rex Rabbit could just chew something dangerous and die. If your pet swallows something toxic, you might not even get a chance to take him to the veterinarian and save him.

This makes it very important to look for areas of hidden dangers and keep the pet safe. These animals have a tendency to chew everything they can. The Mini Rex Rabbit will try to chew anything it can.

It will chew your rugs and carpets. It will chew on rubber items, though such things are very harmful for him. It is you who needs to make sure that the pet does not chew on the wrong items.

It is also important to save your household things from the pet rabbit. You can't let him chew away your favourite carpet or coat. You will have to make sure that your stuff is safe and the pet is also safe.

It is also important to note that if the pet swallows something, blockages can happen easily and they can be very dangerous. There are many rabbits that lose their lives because of such blockages.

Mini Rex Rabbits are so fond of chewing that they will chew on anything. They will chew on rubber items and foam and sponge based products. While they might like chewing on them, these materials when ingested will cause blockage of the digestive tract.

The animal is also very fond of digging tunnels. He will try to dig a tunnel or burrow for itself wherever it can. If you don't pay attention, you might find your rabbit chewing and digging your favourite sofa.

You should understand that he is an animal and wouldn't know what is right or wrong for him. It is you who is responsible for your pet. You have to take measures to avoid such incidents in your home.

Your pet will love digging your sofa and couch. He will try to climb on the furniture and try to chew on the stuffing. He will also not miss an opportunity to chew on paper and plastic items.

These things are extremely dangerous for him if he swallows them. If you don't keep an eye out, your bunny will chew away all your expensive sofas. This is the simple reason why it is expected that the pet is supervised at all times.

Mini Rex Rabbits are also attracted to plants. They will merrily chew on the leaves of various plants. Many house plants are known to be poisonous for the bunny, so they should not be encouraged to eat the leaves.

Additionally, they like digging and tunnelling. So, the animal would try to dig in the sofa material. You should be on the lookout of any tell-tale signs. If you see stuffing material on the floor, you should know what the Mini Rex has been up to. He should be stopped as soon as possible.

If he has been chewing on it, then you know that you will have to keep the bunny away from them. These things are very harmful for the pet. And, it is also very costly for you on the whole.

An animal has a tendency to walk in to a situation and then not know what to do next. He might just climb on to the top of a closet, not knowing what to do.

Rabbits will also crawl into any opening they see. For example, the pet might get under the small opening of a fridge or refrigerator. This is very dangerous because the fan of the fridge can harm him.

Similarly, washing machines and dish washers are potential dangers to the animal. The best way to keep your pet animal out of danger is to know where he is and what he is up to. This will mean that you can help him if he has landed himself into some kind of danger.

You need to be cautious when you are using store bought detergents and bleaching powder to clean surfaces and washrooms. If they have poisonous and toxic ingredients, they can be harmful for the bunny.

To be on the safer side, you should always rinse the surfaces with excess water. This will make sure that the detergent has been washed off. Make sure that the pet does not have access to such harmful things.

There could be so many things in your house that don't look dangerous, but could be very dangerous for your rabbit. This is the reason that you might have to monitor the pet animal when he is not in his cage.

It is also a good idea to designate a spare room in the house for the Mini Rex Rabbit. This room should be open and spacious. It should have natural light and good ventilation.

You can leave the Mini Rex Rabbit in the room and be sure that he is playing and having a good time. Of course, this will totally depend on whether you can spare a room in the house or not.

2. Blocking off dangerous areas

There is no use crying after the damage has been done. It is always better to take the necessary precautions in the very beginning. You should understand the various tendencies of the Mini Rex Rabbit that can pose harm to him.

It is always a good idea to block off dangerous areas. This will mean that the Mini Rex Rabbit will not be able to enter these areas, and you will be able to avoid any kind of mishaps.

You can use barriers to make sure that the Mini Rex Rabbit can't reach certain spots and rooms in the house. But, a point that needs to be noted here is that good quality barriers will have to be used.

You should know that a Mini Rex Rabbit can jump a long distance. So, blocking off areas should be done keeping this in mind. While they can easily jump off bookshelves, they can also squeeze behind one.

Puppy pens and baby gates are two options that you can consider while you are looking for ways to block off certain areas of the house. You can easily find them online or from a store.

Make sure that you make a list of all the areas in the house that you want to block from the bunny. You can choose to block a complete room or certain sections. You should know where you don't want your pet.

It is a good idea to make sure that the barriers are made of good quality metal. This will ensure that the bunny can't chew on it. The last thing that you would want is the Mini Rex chewing off the barriers that were meant to block him.

You should make sure that the right kinds of barriers are used. This is because your naughty Mini Rex Rabbit will happily climb small barriers. He might even get his head stuck in the barrier openings, inviting more trouble for himself and for you also.

If you don't want to invest in high end barriers, then you can look for cheaper alternatives. You can find different kinds of barriers online. Or, you could get these barriers from a shop. They will help to solve your purpose and will be easier on your pocket.

These barriers have a very strong base of plastic. The plastic is good quality and also non-toxic. Barriers made of Plexiglas will also serve the purpose right.

You can make safe and secure barriers on your own. If you wish to make the barrier at your home, then you can use wood. Make sure that you understand how you need to make them.

You can also take some measures to keep the pet bunny away from your furniture. This is important so that they don't try to create a tunnel by chewing on the fabric.

You can also use a good piece of cardboard as a barrier. You can fix some heavy material of cardboard at the bottom end of the furniture that you are trying to protect. This is a relatively non expensive way of protecting your furniture.

To keep the rabbit away from the fridge or refrigerator, you can fix the cardboard in the opening. This will prevent the pet from entering the opening. Make sure you use a good quality cardboard.

This can prevent the pet from digging on the material of the furniture. You can also keep such barriers in front of various rooms. This will make sure that the pet can't enter these rooms. These are simple ways to keep the pet safe and also your things safe.

If you have recliners in your house, keep them away from the pet. The pet could be severely injured by these reclining chairs. The reclining action and the spring could injure the pet, especially the younger bunnies.

To be on the safer side, always check the chair or sofa that you are about to sit on. You don't want to sit on your bunny and injure him. Make sure he is not hiding under tables and sofas.

3. Keeping the Mini Rex away from house plants

You might be shocked to know that many varieties of plants are actually toxic to Mini Rex Rabbits. Your rabbit doesn't know this and he mind end up eating the most toxic plants.

Plants such as tulips and holly are extremely toxic for the Mini Rex Rabbit. There are many other house plants that are poisonous for the Mini Rex. You should try to keep the bunny away from all kinds of house plants.

The best thing to do will obviously be to keep the plants in an area where the pet Mini Rex Rabbit can't reach them. This is a fool proof way to keep them away from the plants.

If you find your beloved pet chewing on some house plant, you should stop him from doing so. It is a good idea to take him to the vet immediately to make sure that he is safe and sound.

4. Keeping dangerous things off limits

If you observe the pet closely, you will start understanding his likes and preferences. After you have kept an eye on him for a few days, you will start understanding his favourite spots in the house.

You will know which areas he likes to dig and where he prefers to hide. These pieces of information can help you to bunny proof your home in a better way.

To begin with, you should make sure that all liquid chemicals are far away from the Mini Rex Rabbit. If a chemical is in reach of the pet, he might accidently spill it all over him.

The bunny can even drink the chemical accidentally. Make sure that the bottles are always closed. To make sure that nothing of the sort happens, you should make sure that all such supplies are kept in top cabinets where the pet can't reach.

Keep away your shoes in a cupboard or cabinet. Before you know, your rabbit might start chewing them. You should also check the bedding, furniture and other things on a regular basis.

You would be surprised to know that your pet can climb cabinets and cupboards. He might jump from high surfaces and might hurt himself in the process. You need to make sure that the rabbit is not up to such mischief.

You should also make sure that all kind of medicines, syrups and tablets are out of the reach of the Mini Rex Rabbit. The pet might just swallow a tablet that it finds on the ground or table. He will not know that this is potential danger.

These can be very harmful for the pet. You can also get childproof cabinets in your home to keep all such potentially dangerous stuff in those cabinets.

You should also exercise precaution near toilets and washrooms. The Mini Rex Rabbit can easily climb toilet seats and cabinets. Just imagine what can happen if the seat is not kept down.

The rabbit can slip or jump inside and can get himself hurt. To avert any such incident, make sure that the toilet seat is kept down. This should be especially done when the Mini Rex is around the toilet area.

You can also keep the toilet door closed to make sure that he does not enter the toilet. If there are any areas of the house that the pet needs to keep away from, you have to keep them closed and blocked. If you don't do so, the pet can just enter the space when you are not around.

The bunny might accidentally swallow the small or shredded pieces. Make sure that the toys that you allow the pet to play with are of good quality. They should be safe for the rabbit, and they should be impossible to swallow for the Mini Rex.

Rubber items can also be very dangerous if they are swallowed by the pet animal. Imagine the kind of damage a rubber band can do if the pet swallows it. You should know that the pet will not know what he is not supposed to do.

You will have to keep him away from danger. You might take some time figuring out how to do things, but once you have it sorted, it will only get easier from there.

Your Mini Rex Rabbit could actually shock you with the kind of things it can get hurt from. He might hurt himself while hopping from one chair to another or while chewing things.

You should make sure any such potentially dangerous things are out of the reach of the bunny. Keep the waste bin and waste stuff away from him because he might try to play with things that could be harmful for him.

You should make sure that the pet sleeps in his cage. This is for his safety and also for the good of the family members. You can also keep him in the cage when you can't supervise him and his actions.

You should make sure that the pet plays with the right kind of toys. Cheap plastic materials that can have an adverse effect on the health of the pet must be avoided. Similarly, toys that can be shredded or broken should also be avoided.

This might be very difficult for you in the beginning to look into areas and places that have hidden dangers for the pet. But, you will definitely learn with time and experience.

The furniture in the house should be pet-friendly. You should make sure there are no sharp edges that could hurt the animal. This will help the bunny to be safe when he is playing around.

Your Mini Rex Rabbit could climb onto the washing machine and dish washer. So, make sure that these items always have a lid on. To be on the safer side, always check inside the washing machine and the dish washer before operating them.

The pet rabbit should stay away from the plants of the house. You should also make sure that he stays away from Styrofoam products. The pet could bite into them and swallow them. This can be potentially very dangerous.

Keep away all rubber products so that the pet can't reach them. This includes both soft rubber and foam rubber products. They can be very harmful if the pet swallows them.

You should also make sure that soaps and detergents are kept away from the reach of the pet. These items can be very dangerous for the pet. The Mini Rex Rabbit could climb up counters and reach such things.

It is better to use the cabinets of bathrooms and rooms to keep things away from the pet rabbit. This will ensure that the pet can't reach them and can't harm himself.

You should make sure that the pet stays away from your clothes. He might chew them away. Always keep the clothes in the cupboards. Never leave them lying around the house. This is like an invitation for the bunny.

Keep the cupboards locked and keep the laundry area closed and locked. If the rabbit gets inside a stack of clothes, it will be a party for him. He will dig tunnels and chew things.

Chapter 6: Diet requirements of the Mini Rex Rabbit

There is no denying the fact that the diet is the one of the most important factors that contributes to the growth of an animal. You have to make sure that your pet animal gets optimum nutrition at all times. This will keep him in the prime of his health.

If your Mini Rex Rabbit is well fed, you will see the positive effects on his health, his mood and his general behaviour. The kind and type of food that he eats will have an effect on all the other aspects of his well-being and his life. Taking care of your pet's diet should always be a priority for you.

The rabbit will have certain natural inclinations based on his habitat and history. You should make an attempt to understand these natural inclinations of the animal. This will help you to plan this food.

You should make all possible efforts to understand the basic requirements of your pet animal. There are a few basic requirements that you will have to fulfil. If you take care of the diet requirements of the Mini Rex Rabbit, you automatically take care of many other aspects.

If your pet is eating tasty and nutritious food, he will be healthy, disease free, stress free and happy. So, it is important that you make all the efforts to make sure that the pet is getting his daily dose of nutrition and health. This is your responsibility as the owner of the pet.

The Mini Rex Rabbit needs a diet that is rich in protein and fibre. The rabbits need the high amounts of protein to supplement the growth of fur. You can see a decrease in the quantity and quality of fur in a Mini Rex Rabbit who is not fed high amounts of protein.

Along with the high amount of protein, the diet should also contain good amounts of fibre. The high amounts of fibre will help in saving the Mini Rex Rabbit from wool block. The fibre is also good for general digestion of the animal.

Sometimes, the rabbit can swallow some hair by mistake. The fibre in the diet of the pet will help him to avoid any harmful consequences because of the swallowing of the hair.

In the wild, these animals would generally feed on hay and grass. So, the food that you should serve to your pet bunny should mainly consist of hay, grass, oat hay and timothy hay.

The pet Mini Rex should also be served green leaves as a part of his diet. The ideal food of the pet would consist of a generous helping of dark green leaves along with good amount of hay or timothy.

To give the Mini Rex Rabbit optimal nutrition, you should also serve him pellets that are commercially available. This will help him to get all rounded nutrition. Some owners also add sunflower seeds to rabbit food because this is good for digestion.

The Mini Rex Rabbits can be given these pellets to give him a good supply of nutrients. There are a few nutrients that are absent in the staple diet of the Mini Rex Rabbit, which is the grass. This can affect his health.

The commercially available pellets can help the pet rabbit to gain those absent nutrients. These nutrients will help in the overall growth of the pet.

If you are looking to buy commercial pellets to supplement the diet of the Mini Rex Rabbit, then you should make sure that the commercial pellets have about 17-20 per cent of protein in them.

These pellets should also contain good amounts of fibre in them. Make sure that you check the percentage of both the protein and fibre in the commercial pellets before deciding to give them to your pet rabbit.

You can easily buy the commercial pellets and other supplements online. They will be delivered to your home in no time. You can also buy them from local feed stores and pet shops. They are easily available these days.

It should be noted that you should always introduce new foods and fruits to the Mini Rex as early as possible. If the pet is young, it is easier for him to acquire the taste.

If you serve vegetables and fruits along with the green leaves, hay and pellets to the Mini Rex Rabbit, you can be sure that your pet is getting the required nutrition from his food.

1. Nutritional requirements of the Mini Rex Rabbit

In the wild, Mini Rex Rabbits are grazers. Their staple diet in the open lands is the grass. The bunnies will hop and walk around and graze on grass in the wild. As the various seasons change, the grazing capacity of these animals also changes.

The food habits of captive bunnies vary slightly from the wild bunnies. The captive Mini Rex are confined in an area and don't have the independence to move around and graze on their favourite grass. But, their diet is not drastically different from the wild ones.

As the owner of the pet, you have to make sure that the pet gets to eat what he ate in his natural habitat. But, along with that other foods should also be introduced to him. This section will help you to understand the types of food you can serve to your Mini Rex pet.

Diet is the most important factor that contributes to the growth of an animal. If your Mini Rex Rabbit is well fed, you will the positive effects in his health, his mood and his general behaviour. So, taking care of your pet's diet should be a priority for you.

Another important point when deciding and finally buying the various food types for your pet is that a pet is totally dependent on you for its needs. It won't be able to tell you that the food is good or bad in quality.

As the chief caregiver of the pet Mini Rex Rabbit, it is your duty to make sure that the food is of the highest quality. You should avoid buying any low quality food just to save some money.

If you are looking for food options, then the following foods can be introduced in the diet of your beloved pet:

- **Grass**: Rabbits love their grass. This is what they feed on in the wild. If you leave them in a garden, they will happily graze on the grass. Grass would be your most natural choice of primary food for your pet Mini Rex Rabbit.

- **Grains:** You can include grains in the diet of the pet bunny. This will add to the quality of the food. Grains are known to be very healthy. They are as good for Mini Rex Rabbits as for human beings. You should make sure that the grain that you serve the pet with is not sweetened and is natural. You can include them in the diet of your pet Mini Rex Rabbit. There are many kinds of grains that you can include in the diet of the pet bunny, such as wheat, milo, oats, millet and barley. These grains can be bought easily from a local store. They will surely make the food of your pet tastier and healthier.

- **Carrots**: You can introduce carrots in the pet's diet. The best way to serve it is the natural form. The carrot is easy to feed and also easy to eat. Carrots are juicy vegetables and have a good content of water. They will also provide the necessary fibre to the Mini Rex.

- **Sweet potatoes**: You should always try to keep the diet of the Mini Rex as natural as possible. It is always better to give the animal some vegetables. The pet will enjoy these vegetables, and in addition to that they will be very healthy. Sweet potato is another option if you are looking for options to introduce in your pet's diet.

- **Apples:** You can also serve fruits to your pets. It is known that the Mini Rex Rabbits enjoy eating certain fruits, such as apples. You can give the bunny apple leaves, fruit and twigs. You can also serve cut fruits or small fruits to the pet animal. If you don't want to serve the apples everyday then you can alternate them with some other food types. Fruits are tasty and have many nutrients. This will have a positive benefit of the health of the pet animal. It should be noted that you should remove the seeds of the fruits before serving them to the Mini Rex Rabbit.

- **Melons:** You can also serve melons to your Mini Rex Rabbit. It is known that the Mini Rex Rabbits enjoy eating these fruits. You can cut these fruits into small pieces before serving them to the rabbit, so that it is easier for the pet to chew. This will have a positive benefit on the health of the pet animal. It should be noted that these fruit types have a very high content of sugar. This can be harmful for the Mini Rex. So, make sure that you serve these fruits to the Mini Rex Rabbit, but in limited quantities. It should be noted that you should remove the seeds of the fruits before serving them to the Mini Rex Rabbit.

- **Alder:** You can also serve alder to the pet. If you don't want to serve them every day then you can alternate them with some other food type. This food type is inherently juicy and has a good content of water. This will also provide the necessary fibre to the pet rabbit.

- **Asparagus:** You can also serve asparagus celery to the Mini Rex Rabbit. If you don't want to serve this food type every day then you can alternate with some other food type.

- **Basil:** You can introduce basil in the pet's diet. The best way to serve it is the natural form. The basil is easy to feed and also easy to eat.

- **Cilantro:** You can include cilantro in the diet of the pet bunny. This will add to the quality of the food. It is known to be very healthy. This food type has a good content of water. This will also provide water to the pet rabbit.

- **Mango and banana:** You can also serve mango and bananas to your Mini Rex Rabbit. It is known that the Mini Rex Rabbits enjoy eating these fruits. You can cut these fruits into small pieces before serving them to the rabbit, so that it is easier for the pet to chew. You can easily serve these fruits once or twice a week. Mangos and bananas are tasty and have many nutrients. This will have a positive benefit of the health of the pet animal. It should be noted that these fruit types have very high content of sugar. This can be harmful for the Mini Rex. So, make sure that you serve mangos and bananas to the Mini Rex Rabbit, but in limited quantities.

- **Wild rye, wild lettuce, mint, horse nettle, grape leaves and vines, catnip, broccoli leaves, beet tops:** You can also serve these to your pet Mini Rex Rabbit, but in limited quantities.

It is known that grass and hay is the chief food required for the Mini Rex Rabbit. When we talk about hay, we are mainly talking about alfalfa hay and timothy hay. Alfalfa hay is known to have high amounts of fibre in it.

The hay should be dry, but should also be soft. Soft and dry hay is the perfect meal for the Mini Rex Rabbit. It is good for the gums of the animal and is also good for the digestive tract and stomach of the animal.

The pet should be encouraged to eat fresh foods. This is good for the digestive system of the pet and his health in general. Make sure that you don't serve him stale vegetables and fruits.

You can easily add hay to the daily diet of the pet Mini Rex Rabbit. Fibre is very important for animals such as the Mini Rex Rabbit. Dietary fibre is said to assist in the digestion process. A high amount of fibre in the diet is very important for a healthy digestive system.

You will have to watch for sharp pieces in the dried grass or hay. Such pieces will injure the pet. The sharp pieces can hurt the gum and inner lining of the mouth. If such pieces are swallowed, they can harm the digestive tract and the stomach of the pet.

If the animal is able to swallow these sharp pieces, his internal organs can also get damaged. So, make sure that you buy only the best quality food for your pet that is devoid of any harmful objects.

2. Amount of food Mini Rex Rabbits require

As the caregiver of the new Mini Rex Rabbit, owner of the new pet, you might want to give all the love and food that you can to your pet. While it is okay to shower the pet with love, feeding too much food is not healthy.

You should limit the quantity of food that you serve to the pet. This section will help you to understand the right amounts of food quantities that your Mini Rex needs.

You should also note that the rabbit will need different quantities at different stages of his life. A growing bunny's requirements will be different from the requirements of the adult bunny.

Similarly, a pregnant or lactating mother doe will have different requirements. It is critical that you understand the needs of your beloved pet, so that you can serve him the right amounts of food at the right time.

The breed of the Mini Rex Rabbit will also directly affect the food that he should be eating. The size of the rabbit will also be a factor that would need to be considered.

It should be noted that a Mini Rex Rabbit belonging to a larger breed will typically need about six ounces of food in a day. On the other hand, smaller ones will need three to five ounces of the feed.

There are many food types you can choose from, but make sure that you don't serve all the food types on a single day. You will have to mix and match to create the right balance, though there are certain food types that the pet requires daily.

If the Mini Rex Rabbit is served food more than what he requires for a healthy well-being, he will rapidly gain weight. It is important to note that obesity in Mini Rex Rabbits is the major cause of some serious health problems.

An obese Mini Rex Rabbit will have difficulty mating. It is known that obesity drastically reduces the ability to reproduce in Mini Rex Rabbits.

Not only will the bunny face issues in reproducing, the health of the pet will suffer. It is known that an obese pet is likely to die early as compared to a healthy and fit Mini Rex Rabbit.

It is important that the everyday diet of the Mini Rex is able provide it with all the necessary nutrients. The Mini Rex Rabbit needs good amounts of fibre and protein in its diet.

The deficiency of various nutrients can lead to many diseases in the Mini Rex Rabbit. So, it is important that the food items that are served to the Mini Rex Rabbit are rich protein and fibre.

It is important that you keep track of what you are feeding your Mini Rex Rabbit throughout the day. Keep a check on all the vegetables and fruit items that you are serving to the Mini Rex Rabbit.

Never overfeed the Mini Rex Rabbit; else you will have to face many difficulties. You should discuss the exact amount of food that the animal needs from time to time with the veterinarian.

3. Foods to avoid

There are many food types that are not suitable for your Mini Rex Rabbit. You can't randomly give anything to the pet because there are many foods that are dangerous for the animal.

You will have to be very careful when you are planning the diet for your pet Mini Rex. A good diet will help to keep the pet animal healthy and will also protect him from various diseases.

First and foremost, you should always keep the surroundings of the Mini Rex Rabbit clean and tidy. Your bunny will try to eat anything and everything around it. This will have a hazardous effect on his health.

You might find your pet eating the sofa covers or the little toys. You should make sure that small toys and other toxic items are not kept around the animal. The health of the pet is your responsibility.

Sometimes, the children of the house can force the pet animal to consume toxic and unhealthy food items just for fun. This can prove to be fatal for the Mini Rex Rabbit. He can suffer serious consequences.

It is important that you keep a check on what the kids are doing with the pet animal. It is always advised to let the children interact with the Mini Rex Rabbit under an adult's supervision.

Keep the food of the Mini Rex Rabbit fresh, simple and healthy. When you are giving fruits, then you should make sure that it should not have seeds because the seeds can be poisonous for the pet Mini Rex Rabbit.

If you are looking for a comprehensive list of food items that are unhealthy for the Mini Rex Rabbit, then the given list will help you. You should avoid these food items:

- **Caffeine**: You should keep caffeine, such as tea and coffee, away from your beloved pet. Caffeine can cause nausea, diarrhoea and other health related issues in the Mini Rex pet.

- **Chocolates and cocoa beans**: These items are unhealthy for Mini Rex Rabbits, especially for the younger ones. These items can cause extreme restlessness in the pet and can also lead to complications. You should make sure that you keep these food items away from the Mini Rex.

- **Onion and garlic**: These items are unhealthy for Mini Rex Rabbits. You should make sure that you keep these food items away from the Mini Rex.

- **Avocado:** Another food item that is dangerous for the Mini Rex Rabbit is avocado. The digestive system of the animal is not suited to digest this food item. The animal will experience diarrhoea and vomiting after it consumes this food. The animal might also find a difficulty in breathing because of this food item.

- **Cookies, cakes and candies:** These items are unhealthy for Mini Rex Rabbits. You should make sure that you keep these food items away from the Mini Rex.

- **Dairy products:** Dairy products can cause vomiting and body weakness in the pet bunny. In some extreme cases, the pet might also suffer from tremors.

- **Raisins and nuts**: Another food group that is dangerous for the Mini Rex Rabbits are raisins and nuts. You might believe that nuts are healthy foods, so they should be fine for your bunny also. But, this is not true. The digestive system of the bunny is not able to digest the nuts. If a bunny consumes them, he will experience vomiting and body weakness. Raisins can negatively affect the kidneys of the

Mini Rex. If these food items are given for a longer duration, substantial damage is done to the kidneys.

- **Mushrooms:** Mushrooms are unhealthy for Mini Rex Rabbits. They can render a lot of harmful effects on the animal. You should make sure that you keep these food items away from the Mini Rex.

- **Pits and iceberg lettuce:** This is another food type that is dangerous for the Mini Rex Rabbits. The digestive system of the Mini Rex Rabbits is not suited to digest them, so you should always avoid feeding them to the bunnies.

- **Tomatoes and tulips:** These food types are unhealthy for Mini Rex Rabbits. You should make sure that you keep these food items away from the Mini Rex.

In case of a situation where the Mini Rex Rabbit has consumed something that is toxic for him, you should consult the veterinarian as soon as possible. You should not delay matters like these.

You can also contact the 'Pet poison control' authority in severe cases. The number of the 'Pet poison control' is 888-426-4435.

4. Water needs of the bunny

A Mini Rex Rabbit needs good amounts of water for its survival. You should make sure that the animal always has access to drinking water.

Water helps the Mini Rex Rabbit to regulate its body temperature. The rabbit has a thick coat of fur over his body. It is very important that the body of the pet maintains the right temperature.

If the Mini Rex Rabbit is not hydrated well, he can develop severe health complications. You can even lose your pet Mini Rex because of lack of water in his system. To avoid such things, make sure that the pet is hydrated at all times.

You should buy chew proof water bottles for the Mini Rex Rabbits. These bottles can be easily hung in the hutch or cage of the rabbit. These bottles are easily available. You can order them online or can buy from pet shops easily.

If you keep a water container in the hutch or cage of the pet Mini Rex, there is a high probability that the pet will play in the water. Even if he does not play, the water can spill easily in the cage or over the Mini Rex Rabbit.

The water can wet the coat of the Mini Rex Rabbit. It is important that the fur of the Mini Rex Rabbit is always dry. The wet wool is the source of many health issues, especially skin related diseases in the Mini Rex.

The water bottle will allow the pet to easily drink water and will also keep the wool of the pet dry. You should buy such water bottles for the Mini Rex Rabbit.

You should make sure that there is water in the water bottle at all times. You should re-fill the water daily and should also clean the bottle frequently. These are simple way to keep the pet bunny healthy and hydrated.

It is easy to clean these water bottles. There are special brushes available in pet stores and also online that will allow you to clean the water bottles easily and without a fuss. Make sure that you clean them at least once in a week.

You should also make sure that you purchase the right extensions to attach to the water bottle. These extensions will allow you to keep the water bottles in place and will also allow you to fix them at the right angle with the cage of the pet bunny.

If you live in a place where water freezes during winters, you will have to take special care of the Mini Rex Rabbit. You might be busy in your work and all the water in the water bottle could be frozen.

Such a condition can force the pet to go without water for extended periods, which is extremely dangerous for the Mini Rex.

A simple solution to this problem is to use heated bowls in winter. But, with this the same issue of the fur getting wet arises. You will have to be more careful and will have to make sure that the fur of the pet is trimmed regularly.

The trimming will reduce the chances of skin issues because of wet fur. You should try your best to keep the Mini Rex Rabbit safe and dry.

5. Introducing new foods to the Mini Rex Rabbits

When you bring a pet Mini Rex Rabbit home, one of the biggest concerns that you will have is regarding its diet. It would take you time to understand the diet preferences of the new bunny.

The Mini Rex Rabbit will naturally be inclined to eating hay and grass. You should also introduce him to certain vegetables and fruits. This will have a very positive effect in his overall health.

If you want to introduce new foods or switch foods, you can't suddenly change the rabbit's usual meal plan. This will put off the bunny. He might even give up eating the food. This is something that you would never want.

It is suggested that the pet should be introduced to different food types quite early in his life. This will make it easier for you and also for the pet Mini Rex Rabbit. This will help the bunny to have his preferences and will also make things easier for you.

In case a certain food item is not available, you know that you have other choices. If you don't introduce new foods to the pet Mini Rex, he will turn out to be a very fussy eater. And, you will find it very difficult to provide him with the right types of food.

You should slowly introduce new foods to the pet Mini Rex. There are some simple tips and tricks that you should be following to make sure that the pet is eating well even when new foods are being introduced.

You should introduce one new food at a time. A simple way of introducing new food in the diet of the Mini Rex Rabbit is by starting out with a small amount of the food. Take a bowl and add the usual food of the pet in it.

Now, take very small amount of the new food that you wish to feed your pet in the bowl. Mix the contents and serve the food to the pet animal. You should introduce vegetables and fruits in the diet of the Mini Rex Rabbit.

You should remember that the Mini Rex Rabbit needs time to get used to it. But, there is nothing to worry even if the pet leaves the new food in the beginning.

Just keep adding a very small amount of the food item in the usual food of the pet. This might take some time so be prepared for it. Once you see that the pet has started eating the new food along with the usual old food, you can gradually increase the portion of the new food.

The given process will take some days, but you will have to have some patience. The idea is to help the pet to get used to the food before you can expect the pet to eat the food. Once he is gets used to it, he will try out the food item on his own.

6. Commercial pellets

The diet of the Mini Rex Rabbit should be highly nutritious. This will help him in wool production and also to keep him healthy. It is important that you make sure that the rabbit gets daily doses of his nutrition.

The food should contain a good amount of protein, fibre and other nutrients. This will help in providing the Mini Rex Rabbit with most of his nutritional requirements.

Even if you make sure that the Mini Rex Rabbit is getting all its necessary nutrients from the food itself, you can't avoid the use of commercial pellets. At times, your bunny's diet might not be able to provide it with the right set of nutrients and vitamins.

In such a case, it becomes necessary to introduce supplements in the diet of the Mini Rex Rabbit. This ensures that the pet is getting all the necessary vitamins and minerals in his diet. This is important to keep the pet healthy and sound.

If you are looking to buy commercial pellets to supplement the diet of the Mini Rex Rabbit, then you should make sure that the commercial pellets have good amounts of both protein and fibre.

As a rule, you should make sure that the commercial pellets contain 17-20 per cent of protein in them. They should also have about 14-15 per cent of fibre in them. Protein and fibre are essential for the growth of a Mini Rex Rabbit.

There are many vitamin supplements that are available in tasty treat forms for the bunny. While you can be sure that your pet is getting the right nutrients, the pet can enjoy the treat given to him.

If the pet is not well and is recuperating from an injury or disease, the veterinarian might advise you to administer certain supplements to the pet. These supplements will help the pet to heal faster and get back on his feet sooner.

You should always consult a veterinarian before you administer any supplement to the Mini Rex Rabbit. He will be the best judge of which supplements the Mini Rex Rabbit requires and which ones he doesn't.

While it can be necessary to supplement certain vitamins and nutrients to the pet, you should also be aware of the hazards of over-feeding a certain nutrient. If there is an overdose of a certain vitamin in the body of the Mini Rex Rabbit, it can lead to toxicity.

Everything should be given in right quantities and that too at the right time. You can't give him ten pellets at a time and expect him to be healthy. You have to follow a strict schedule to make sure that the pet remains healthy.

You might even see that your pet is enjoying all the supplements, but this in no way means that you can give him an overdose. You should always do what is right for the rabbit's health.

Another point that you should take care of is that you should not blindly follow the instructions and dosage that is printed on various supplements. You should consult the veterinarian to decide the final dosages.

The food that you feed the Mini Rex Rabbit should have a good supply of nutrients, fibre and vitamins. The commercial pellets should only be used to supplement the diet of the pet and to replace the diet.

You can easily buy the commercial pellets and other supplements online. They will be delivered to your home in no time. You can also buy them from local feed stores and pet shops. They are easily available these days.

Chapter 7: Taking care of the Mini Rex Rabbit's health

An unhealthy pet can be a nightmare for any owner. As the prospective owner or the owner of a beautiful Mini Rex Rabbit, you might be thinking about what you can do to ensure that the pet is always in the prime of its health. You can contribute a great deal to the health of the animal.

The food that you provide the animal with, the conditions that you keep him in and the love that you give him will all affect the general well-being and the health of the Mini Rex Rabbit.

You should always make sure that your pet is always kept in a clean environment. A neat and clean environment will help you to keep off many common ailments and diseases. Also, make sure that the pet is well fed at all times.

When you are looking to maintain the health of your pet Mini Rex Rabbit, you should make an attempt to understand the common health issues that the animal faces. This will help you to prepare yourself well and also treat your pet well.

It is important that you take care of your pet's health. The pet will depend on you for most of its needs. It will not be able to tell you if it is facing any discomfort regarding its health. You should be able to identify the symptoms of various diseases in your pet to treat it well.

You should also be able to diagnose any symptoms of injuries in your pet. If you can treat him in your home, then you should do it very carefully. In case you have any doubts, you should take the pet to the veterinarian.

1. Injuries in the Mini Rex Rabbits

As you would have understood by now, your Mini Rex Rabbit is a very mischievous animal. He will lead a very active lifestyle. The pet likes hopping and jumping around. He will also enjoy exploring things.

All the traits of the bunny make it susceptible to many injuries. There is nothing to worry about if your pet animal injures itself. You should be able to diagnose the injuries so that they can be treated well.

Never commit the mistake of ignoring an injury or a symptom. Even if you have the slightest doubt, you should always act on it. It is always a good idea to take the Mini Rex Rabbit to the veterinarian if you spot something unnatural with the pet.

It is important that you learn the basics of diagnosing the injuries. This is important because if a small injury is treated well, the Mini Rex Rabbit can be saved from a major problem in the future.

You should be on the lookout for any symptoms that your Mini Rex Rabbit might display when it is injured. These symptoms could mean that there is something wrong with your bunny.

It is important that you understand that your pet animal might not show any signs of injuries, even when it is injured. It will be your responsibility to diagnose the injury before it turns into a bigger problem.

Understand some basic signs of injuries, stress and diseases in the pet Mini Rex Rabbit. This will help you to get the pet treated on time. If the pet is treated on time, you can avoid many future problems.

Is your pet looking very lazy and lethargic? Is your Mini Rex Rabbit looking very disturbed? This could be because he has injured himself and is in pain.

The pet might injure himself with a chair or other furniture while playing. The limbs of the animal could also be hanging. This is also a clear sign of injury to the pet. You should closely examine his limbs to be sure.

Is your pet stumbling? Is the pet showing uncoordinated movements? If you find these symptoms, then you know that the pet has some kind of issue. Take him on your lap and gently check his limbs.

If there is a change in the way he sits or stands or carries himself, then this could also mean that the injury has forced the pet to change the way he usually is. This could be because he is in pain.

You should look out for the faeces of the animal. If there is any change in the colour of the faeces, this could mean that there is something wrong with the health of the pet.

Do you see any changes in the skin of the pet? If yes, then this could also mean that there is something that needs your attention. Don't overlook anything that does not seem very natural.

Do you spot any blood on the skin of the animal? Does the fur of the pet look different? You should look for blood stains in the enclosure of the animal also. This could mean that something is not right.

Look for certain common symptoms, such as coughing and vomiting in the animal. If your pet looks scared and tensed, you should understand that it is for a reason. You need to closely examine him to find out what is wrong.

When you spot any of the given symptoms in your pet, you should know that something is not right. You will have to take a closer look at the pet and examine. This examination will help you to understand if there is something wrong with your pet.

While you are examining your pet, you should also understand that your pet could be scared. It is important that you make the pet feel comfortable. This will help you conduct the examination properly and without any problems.

To make sure that the pet animal is not terrified when you are trying to examine him for any potential injuries, you should make sure that you conduct the examination in a closed area, a place where the animal feels safe and protected. You should try to examine him indoors.

Make sure that all the tools that are needed for the examination are ready. You shouldn't leave your pet alone to fetch the tools. Everything should be ready before the examination.

The noise level around you should be as low as possible. The noise will stress the pet and will irritate him, so make sure there is no noise around. Conduct the examination in a quiet place. This is important to keep things under control.

Do not let the place be crowded when the examination is being conducted. Make sure that all the other pets and your family members are outside and not in the same place where the examination is being conducted.

If the animal sees you being fidgety, it will only add to his stress. Be as gentle and kind as possible. This will help your pet to relax and feel less stressed. You should in no way add to the stress and pain of the pet.

You should be as calm and as confident as possible. Your confidence will give him some hope and relief. These are some very simple tips, but will go a long way in ensuring that the pet is being handled well.

You should check his entire body. Remember to check on both sides of the body. Start the examination at one particular point and then move ahead from that point. The examination should be definite and guided and not random.

Look at how your pet responds to the body examination being done. If you feel that the animal is not taking it too well, you should stop the examination. You should look for any stress signs that he displays.

It is important that you don't ignore any symptoms. It is also important that you don't force anything on the pet; otherwise the animal can go into deep shock. After your initial check-up, if you find something wrong then visit the veterinarian.

You should never self-treat the pet. This could complicate things further. Take the pet to the veterinarian because he is the best judge of the pet's condition. Discuss your doubts and confusions with the vet.

2. Identifying stress signs and sickness in Mini Rex Rabbits

As the parent of the Mini Rex Rabbit, you should always be very careful about the well-being of the pet. To make sure that the pet is doing well, you should be on the lookout for various sickness and stress signs in the bunny.

There are a few symptoms that will help you to identify stress and sickness in your pet. Examine the behaviour and the body of the pet carefully. This will help you to identify the symptoms.

You should conduct a body examination in case of doubt, and as soon as you spot any of the symptoms, take the pet Mini Rex Rabbit to a qualified and good veterinarian. He will be able to confirm the presence of disease and stress in the animal.

A sick Mini Rex Rabbit will seem very lethargic. The animal will show a drastic change in its activity level. There are a few Mini Rex Rabbits that might get fidgety, while others will become very lethargic. They will not move at all.

The pet will try to escape you when it is stressed. It will not let you come closer to him and will get irritated. The pet might show violent movements. He might get stressed when someone approaches him.

The pet would be seen grinding its teeth tightly and flicking its ears. The pet would be seen shaking his head angrily. You would be able to make out that something is wrong with the pet.

He would make strange and loud noises from his mouth, when not grinding his teeth tightly. If you measure the body temperature of the animal, there will be a change in the body temperature.

The Mini Rex will lose an interest in eating and drinking. He will lose his appetite. This is a signal that something is definitely wrong with the pet. When your bunny is not eating, you need to consult the veterinarian.

If the animal is not treated on time, you will see that his appetite decreases with time. It will decrease to a point that it will become difficult for the animal to carry out his daily tasks.

The animal could also hurt himself. He might claw at himself. The animal could lick his various body parts, such as legs and feet.

The Mini Rex Rabbit could also show the symptom of diarrhoea. He will suffer from frequent and liquid stools. This means that the pet needs your attention and the condition should not be ignored.

At this juncture, you would want to reduce the amount of stress that your Mini Rex Rabbit must be going through. It is important that you take all the necessary steps to make the Mini Rex Rabbit feel safe and secure.

You should keep him securely on a comfortable blanket to make him feel easy and comfortable. This will give him the much needed security and warmth.

Gently wrap the blanket around the pet Mini Rex Rabbit. This is like a reassurance to the animal that he can be safe and secure in the warmth provided by the blanket. If the temperature of the pet is high, you should avoid this step.

If the pet does not react well to your actions, you should take a back seat. It is important that you don't force him to do anything.

You should make sure that your pet can rest well in a calm environment. Keep him away from any place of commotion. Make sure that there are no noises around the rabbit.

Any kind of noises that can startle him will disrupt him and will agitate him. It should be made sure that all the noises are eliminated. This should be avoided at all costs.

Let the pet be easy and on his own. But, be around him so that he knows that he is safe. You should also try your level best to make sure that there are not many people around the pet Mini Rex.

3. Common health problems of the Mini Rex Rabbits

Nobody would want to see a helpless animal suffering from a disease. To make sure that your bunny enjoys good health at all times, it is important that you recognize the symptoms of diseases that can affect a Mini Rex Rabbit at an early stage.

If you can detect a disease in an early stage, there are more chances that the disease will be cured. To be able to do so, you should make an attempt to understand the various diseases that can affect a Mini Rex Rabbit along with their symptoms.

There are many common health issues that your Mini Rex Rabbit is prone to. There are many issues that might not start as a big problem, but become serious problems if not treated on time.

You should also never ignore any symptom that you see because an ignored symptom will lead to serious problems later. As in humans, an early detected problem or disease can be treated easily in pets.

It should be noted that even if your pet is healthy and all seems to be just fine with him, you should make sure that you take him to the vet for periodic visits. This is to make sure that all remains fine.

The vet will examine the health of the pet Mini Rex Rabbit, and will help you to understand if something needs your attention. Such visits will also help in detecting even the slightest issues with the bunny.

There are many diseases that might not start with a big warning. They might become serious diseases if not treated on time. You should also never ignore any symptom that you see because an ignored symptom will lead to serious problems later.

Like most pet animals, the Mini Rex Rabbit is also prone to various kinds of diseases. As the owner and caregiver, you should attempt to understand these diseases in detail, so that you can provide the animal with the right care.

This section will help you to understand the various common health problems that your pet bunny can suffer from.

Coccidiosis

One of the most common health problems in Mini Rex Rabbits is the Coccidiosis. This particular health problem is caused by protozoa Cocci, which have only one single cell.

It is important to know that there are nine types of Cocci that can affect rabbits. Eight out of these nine types are known to affect the intestines of the bunnies. The ninth type of Cocci can affect the liver of the Mini Rex Rabbit.

You should also know that cats, dogs and chickens can also be affected by Cocci. It is also important to note that the young rabbits are often more susceptible to Cocci. So, they need more attention and protection.

The older bunnies have immunity against this disease. So, if you have a young Mini Rex Rabbit, then you should be worried about this health issue. It is important that you understand the causes and ways to avoid this disease.

One of the most common causes of this disease is an unclean area. If the cage or the hutch of the rabbit is not cleaned for days, you can expect your Mini Rex Rabbit to get infected with this disease.

The parasite will dwell in dirty areas. The Mini Rex Rabbit will ingest the egg of the disease causing parasite. They will do so when they lick or eat from dirty cage floors or when they eat contaminated hay.

While the adult rabbit is less likely to suffer from this condition, it can be a carrier. It can shed away the eggs of the parasite in its faeces. This can further infect other pet Mini Rex Rabbits in the vicinity.

The eggs of this disease causing parasite can thrive and survive for over a year in a humid and warm place. This makes it all the more important that you regularly clean the surroundings of the Mini Rex Rabbit.

Symptoms:

You can look out for the following symptoms in the bunny to know that he is suffering from this particular disease:

- The pet will lose his appetite. You will find him avoiding even his favourite foods. He will not drink water, which could further lead to dehydration.

- You will notice a sudden and drastic weight loss in the pet. This is one of the most common symptoms of this condition.

- Another symptom of this disorder is vomiting. The pet will throw up from time to time.

- The pet would be seen struggling during his bowel movements. You should watch out for this symptom.

- You will notice the bunny to be very lazy and lethargic.

- You can spot your Mini Rex Rabbit sitting in one corner with a hunched back. His feet will be forward, and he will appear to be really sad and sick.

- The pet will suffer from diarrhoea. You might also notice blood in the stools of the Mini Rex Rabbit.

Treatment:

If you find any of the above symptoms in a Mini Rex Rabbit, it is important that you waste no time and take the pet to the veterinarian. The vet will conduct some tests to confirm the condition.

The most common treatment of this condition includes the use of corid powder. You can get it easily at all pet stores. Sulfamethoxide is also used to help the pet recover from this condition.

It should be mixed with water and given to the pet Mini Rex Rabbit for seven days. After the first cycle, a break of over seven days is taken. After that, the mix needs to be given for another seven days.

Most veterinarians will suggest completing these two cycles at least once in six months. This ensures that the Mini Rex Rabbit does not get this health condition. This is all the more important in young bunnies.

If your female bunny is pregnant, you should not administer this particular drug to the doe. It can be given to her once she is in the lactating phase.

Usually the symptoms of this disease start with the pet being lazy and losing his appetite. The other symptoms might not show for a very long time. The best way to avoid this disease is to take the necessary precautions.

It is important that you don't ignore any symptom and consult the vet as soon as possible. Always try to maintain cleanliness in the hutch of the pet Mini Rex Rabbit.

Ringworms

Ringworms are a very common issue that can affect your pet rabbit. Ringworms can attach themselves to the Mini Rex Rabbit. This will cause immense discomfort to the Mini Rex Rabbit.

While many people don't consider this as a major health issue, ringworms should never be ignored. They are known to be very dangerous. They can be a potential threat to your other pets also. You should make sure that ringworms are treated well and that too on time.

If you believe that ringworm is a worm, then you are wrong. It is a fungus and fungal treatment is required to get rid of the ringworms. If you are treating your pet for worms, then you will not be able to combat this condition.

The problem with this disease is that it can get worse with time. So, it is important that you treat it as soon as possible. If the ringworms are allowed to grow on the animal, they will lead to a lot of fur loss.

There are many causes that could be behind the ringworms attacking your pet. One of the most common causes of ringworms is the contact with animals already infested with the same.

Ringworms can easily travel from one carrier to the other. So, if an animal infested with the ringworms comes in contact with your Mini Rex, he can easily get them too.

Symptoms:

You should be on the lookout of the following symptoms to confirm the presence of ringworms on your Mini Rex Rabbit:

- Is your Mini Rex Rabbit scratching itself too much? Does your pet seem as if he has an itch? Do you see some areas red with itchiness and scratching?

- Do you find him irritable and uneasy? If the answer is yes, then your Mini Rex Rabbit could be infected by ringworms.

- Ringworms make the animal itchy and too much itchiness can develop red sores on the body. You should be on the lookout for such obvious symptoms of ringworms.

- The pet will slowly develop bald patches. You should be on the lookout for this symptom. It is one of the most common symptoms of the Mini Rex Rabbit being infected by ringworms.

- The head of the Mini Rex is most likely to be affected. It will slowly spread to other parts of the body. You should look out for bald patches on the head.

Treatment:

If you find the given symptoms on your pet then you can be convinced that your pet has been infested by ringworms. It is important that you take the steps to help your pet get rid of them.

If you do not treat the pet soon, then they will only trouble the poor animal more. You can successfully treat the ringworms in following an antifungal treatment for the condition.

You should not allow the pet to come into contact with other pets of the house. The ringworms can spread very easily. Human beings can also easily catch them. You should wear gloves when you go near the pet Mini Rex.

If you find any of the above symptoms in a Mini Rex Rabbit, it is important that you waste no time and take the pet to the veterinarian. The vet will conduct some tests to confirm the condition.

He will suggest an antifungal cream that will help to get rid of the ringworms. The fur in the affected area needs to be tied so that the ringworms don't spread to other parts of the body.

Salmonellosis

The Salmonella bacteria is said to affect the Mini Rex Rabbit and cause this condition. It is also called as Scours in the Mini Rex Rabbits. This condition is characterized by excessive diarrhoea.

The main reasons behind this condition of Salmonellosis are unhealthy diet and poor hygiene conditions. If you give your bunny a proper and healthy diet and also try to maintain optimal hygiene conditions around him, you can definitely avoid this health condition in the pet.

If the pet animal is suffering from a severe case of viral or bacterial infection, scours could be one of the side effects of the infection. In such cases, it is best to treat the infection if you want to treat this condition.

There are various causes that could be behind the scours in your pet animal. One of the most common causes of Salmonellosis or scours in your Mini Rex is lack of a healthy diet. You have to make sure that your pet is fed properly so that it can be in its optimum health and glory.

If you feed excessive food to your pet, much of the food can go undigested. This will hamper his digestive system and bowel movements. One of the effects of such a condition is scours.

Another common cause of this health condition in bunnies is stress and over-heating. When your pet is going through excessive stress, it will lead to scours.

If there is poor hygiene around the pet Mini Rex, it can also lead to Salmonellosis or scours. You should try to maintain optimum hygiene levels at all times.

If the pet is suffering from some other infection or health condition, scours could be a side effect of the health condition.

Symptoms:

There are certain symptoms that will help you to diagnose whether your pet animal has scours or not. In case you find the symptoms, you should make it a point to treat his condition well. You can also take your pet to the vet.

The following symptoms will help you to confirm whether your pet is suffering from this health condition:

- One of the early symptoms of this disease includes diarrhoea. If your pet is suffering from diarrhoea that you are not able to control, then your pet could be suffering from scours.

- You should keep a check on the stools of the rabbit. The colour and texture of the stools will help you determine whether the rabbit has Salmonellosis or not.

- Does your pet suffer from liquid stools? If yes, then this could be a clear case of scours.

- Is your pet passing frequent stools? This could be because of an infection, poor hygiene or improper food.

Treatment:

If your pet is suffering from Salmonellosis, you would have to take certain measures to solve this issue. But you don't need to worry as it can be treated. It is advised to administer probiotics to the animal. This will help to treat his condition.

He should be given electrolytes. The electrolytes will help to give the body the salts that it might have lost because of the condition.

Once your pet starts getting better, you should make sure that it is given a very healthy diet. A good diet is the precaution of Salmonellosis. Make sure that all the necessary nutrients are given to the pet. You can also look to give him supplements if his diet does not provide the right nutrition.

You can even consult your veterinarian if your pet doesn't get better. The medication given by the doctor will help the pet to get better quickly.

Pneumonia

The Mini Rex Rabbit is also highly susceptible to pneumonia, especially when the bunny is young. If your Mini Rex shows symptoms of a respiratory disorder, then you should look for various symptoms of this disease.

It can be caused by bacteria that thrive in dirty and unsanitary conditions. This is the reason why it is always advised to keep the hutches clean and sanitary.

The main cause of this health condition is damp hutches and cages. If the living conditions of the pet are not good, he can suffer from this disease.

It is important that you treat this disease because it is known to be a life threating condition. If you discover any respiratory disorders in your pet, you should take the issue seriously because as the disease reaches its advanced stages, it becomes more difficult to treat.

Symptoms:

You should be on the lookout for the following symptoms to confirm the presence of the disease in your Mini Rex Rabbit:

- If your pet animal refuses to eat, then this could be because of this disease. The pet will suffer a drastic loss of appetite.

- Is your pet being very lazy and lethargic? Is he refusing to move? This could also be because of this disease.

- The pet Mini Rex will have difficulty breathing. There could be a blockage or congestion in the chest area. This is a very common symptom and should be taken very seriously.

- The pet could be suffering from a high temperature. This is also a very common symptom accompanying pneumonia.

- The pet might vomit the food that he is fed. This is because of the congestion in his chest.

Treatment:

There is treatment available if your Mini Rex Rabbit is suffering from pneumonia. The type of treatment that will be chosen will depend on a few factors. If the pneumonia is too severe, then a different treatment is chosen in comparison to if it is not too severe.

The vet will recommend antibiotics to combat the disease. The dose and strength of the antibiotic will depend on the severity of pneumonia in the pet bunny.

If the bunny is not able to recover and is already at an advanced stage, then the dose of antibiotic is injected directly through the skin. This is known to work rapidly on the animal.

Chapter 8: Training and Grooming the Mini Rex Rabbit

When you decide to keep a Mini Rex Rabbit as a pet, you should understand that your Mini Rex Rabbits are smart and intelligent animals. You will find it easier to train them to stay in a household.

By nature, animals can be unpredictable. So, efforts and planning at your end are important. This training phase will also require you to be patient. You will have to do a few trial and errors before you can be sure that your pet is well trained.

It is very important to train the animal to make him more suitable to a household. You should remember to have fun even during the training phase. You shouldn't be too harsh on your pet. Give him some time and show some patience. He will get there before you know it.

The most important point that you need to remember when you are training your pet is that it is not possible to train the Mini Rex Rabbit in just a few steps. The bunny will forget and go back to his basic habits if you are not consistent.

You will have to do the same steps again and again. These repetitive actions will require patience and time. It may take weeks or months before you see any positive results. If you don't see instant results, don't get angry, and don't hit the animal.

Pets are like small children. You have to deal with them with patience and love. If you beat your bunny out of frustration, you will rupture the bond between the two of you. He will detest coming to you and things will only get worse.

If you think that punishing the pet will help to train him, then you should understand that the pet might not even realize which actions are leading to the punishment. It will only confuse him further. When you hit him, there is a great chance that he will be physically hurt.

You can also injure the pet severely. The pet might slip into sadness and depression if severe training sessions continue. This will hamper the pet's emotional bond with you and also his health. You should refrain from doing so.

When you are training the pet, try not to chase him. Rabbits generally associate chasing with being held captive. If you wish to play with them, kneel on the floor. You should be on the same level as the rabbit if you wish him to enjoy playing with you.

They will play in your arms for some time and then will want to come down. You should be prepared for such behaviour from your pet. Let him be the way he wishes to be. This will allow him to get comfortable in your presence.

The training phase can be a great opportunity for you to learn more about your little pet. No matter how much you read about an animal, your pet will have some individual properties that will separate him from the rest of the lot. This is a good time to learn about all these properties.

1. Is it possible to train a Mini Rex Rabbit?

You would definitely want the pet to be well trained and behaved. The Mini Rex Rabbit is used to being in the wild on its own. If you wish to domesticate it, you have to tame it. If you wish to tame it, you will have to rely on some training skills to do so.

It is imperative to train a pet. This is a simple way to monitor their behaviour and to teach them what behaviour is acceptable and what isn't. You should adopt simple training techniques to train your Mini Rex Rabbit. If you are consistent, you will get very good results.

Many of you might be wondering whether a Mini Rex Rabbit can actually be trained, if he is so mischievous and playful. The truth is that they can be trained. You will be required to put in more time and effort to do so.

You should not make the mistake of starting the training of the Mini Rex Rabbit when he is too old. You should not wait up until then. The sooner you start the training, the better it is. You should start the training when the rabbit is very young. In fact, you should start the training soon after you bring him home.

You should understand the importance of training the pet animal. The Mini Rex needs to be taught certain things so that it does not get back to his basic wild behaviour. Apart from teaching him the right behaviour, training will also help to form a bond between you and your pet. It will bring the two of you closer to each other.

If you start the training of the pet from a young age then this will give the pet some time to learn and understand what is expected out of him. It is also important that the training is not stopped at any stage. Once you see him picking up, reduce the intensity but don't stop the training.

Your Mini Rex Rabbit can be trained for many things, such as bath training and litter training. Training the pet is an important part of bringing up a pet in the household. This is a simple way of helping him adapt to your home and your family.

When you are training your pet animal, you need to teach him what is acceptable and what is not. This might be difficult for you in the beginning. When you are training the animal, you need to be aware of his basic nature. This will help you to bring in the right changes in your training techniques.

It is important to send the right signals to the pet. This is a way of teaching him as to what is expected of him and what is not. The pet will take some time, but will soon understand your instructions.

If your pet comes in a mode where he tries to bite you continuously then you should give a small toy to the pet. Let him bite the toy. You should repeat this action whenever he tries to bite you. This will send a signal to the pet animal that it is not okay for him to bite you.

The more you learn about your pet, the stronger bond you form with him. You should remember to not take the training phase as a cumbersome thing. In fact, take it as an opportunity to form an everlasting bond with your pet. Your pet will also understand you better during this time.

While you have to be regular and stern during this phase, you should not be harsh and rude. Don't beat the poor rabbit. You will only scare the pet and jeopardize your relationship with him. If you have your doubts, it is better to read more about them and then take your decisions regarding the bunny's training phase.

When you are looking at training the Mini Rex Rabbit, you should be aiming for litter training and training against chewing and biting above everything else. These trainings are important to help the bunny adjust into the household and also to make things easier for you and your family.

While you are training your pet, you should remember that the Mini Rex Rabbit needs to feel comfortable and secure in your presence. You should spend quality time with him. Don't put him in the cage unnecessarily.

If he is left in the cage unattended all the time, he will become very aggressive. This will encourage his chewing and biting behaviour. Always remember that they can bite when they are scared and disappointed.

You should never neglect your pet. The Mini Rex Rabbit will learn slowly, but you have to be compassionate and kind towards the pet. Treat him when he exhibits good behaviour. This will encourage him further.

2. Litter training

As the owner, you are also the care taker and the parent for the pet. You will have to teach him stuff that he needs to know when living in a family. Don't get upset when you see your Mini Rex Rabbit littering all around. You can train him not to do so.

To begin with, you should buy a few litter boxes. Keep these boxes in various areas of the house where the Mini Rex Rabbit is most likely to litter. You should signal the Mini Rex Rabbit by pointing towards the litter box.

The pet should slowly realize that he needs to use the box if he wants to get out of the cage. You should wait near the cage till he is all done.

You should cover the various corners where you have found the litter earlier. Also, install one box in the cage. Eventually, you want the Mini Rex Rabbit to litter in the cage itself.

If you notice that the pet is not using the litter box installed in his cage, then you need to understand why. There is a chance that the litter box is uncomfortable for him. In such a case, you should look to buy a comfortable litter box.

Another point that you need to understand here is that Mini Rex Rabbit is very smart. When the Mini Rex Rabbit understands that you will let him out of the cage once he uses the litter box, he might pretend to use it. You need to check the box and make sure that he has actually used it.

The Mini Rex Rabbit will take its own good time to adjust to the environment. It is always difficult for a new pet to adjust. If you get him a new cage or if you make any changes in his surroundings, he will find it difficult to adjust.

But, this problem is only time related and will get solved. Every time the Mini Rex Rabbit litters outside the box, place his litter in the box that he should be using.

You need to show the pet that he should be using the litter box. This could be difficult for you in the beginning, but the Mini Rex Rabbit will learn soon. You should place food and toys in areas and corners that you want to save.

You can also place a mat underneath the litter box to save your carpet or home mats. Make sure that the mat that you use is water proof.

The litter box of the Mini Rex Rabbit should definitely be kept clean to maintain the overall hygiene and to prevent diseases. You should wash the box once a week.

Observe your Mini Rex Rabbit's mannerisms when he is using the litter box. If he has a tendency to bite the mat underneath or stuff kept around, you should discourage this behaviour. To do so, you can use the bitter food sprays on the mats and other stuff. This will automatically discourage the pet from biting around when he is littering.

You should leave some organic paper litter in the box to encourage the pet to use the box again. This is a simple trick that you can use when you are trying to litter train your pet.

This paper litter can be bought very easily. It will help you to make the Mini Rex Rabbit use the litter box. You can cover the litter with some hay.

When you are buying a litter box, you should remember that the size of the box will depend on the size of your Mini Rex Rabbit. For example, a bigger Mini Rex Rabbit will need a bigger box due to his size as compared to the box that a smaller breed Mini Rex Rabbit will need.

If you are domesticating more than one Mini Rex Rabbit in your home, then this will also affect the littering process of the Mini Rex Rabbits. This may come as a surprise to you, but the dominant pet could affect how the other pets use the litter boxes in the house.

You might notice that the habits of a dominant pet Mini Rex Rabbit are influencing the other pet Mini Rex Rabbits. The dominant one will always try to boss around and make the others feel inferior.

You should make sure that each Mini Rex Rabbit has his own box, so that he not left to use the carpets and the floors. Even after you have trained your Mini Rex Rabbit to use the litter box, you have to be vigilant.

If you are observant, you might have to face issues. There could be instances when your pet Mini Rex Rabbit would suddenly give up the use of the litter box. Instead of getting angry with him, it is important that you probe into the reason for his sudden change in behaviour.

When the Mini Rex Rabbit is sick, he might give up the use of the litter box. The main reason behind this is that the pet might not have the strength in his hind legs to get on to the box. He could be suffering from a disease, which could make him weak and lethargic.

You should be cautious when you observe such changes in your pet Mini Rex Rabbit. Don't ignore his condition, or don't force him to use the litter box. You should not get angry with the pet because he is littering on the floor. It is not his fault if he is not well.

The best thing to do in such a situation is to take the pet to the vet. This will avoid the condition getting worse. He will look for the symptoms of various diseases and will help you to understand what is wrong with the pet.

3. Training the pet against chewing and biting

When you buy a new Mini Rex Rabbit, you might notice that the animal has a tendency to bite things. This is a very natural behaviour of a rabbit. They try to bite and chew everything. So, you shouldn't be very surprised.

You will see him trying to chew everything he can, such as furniture and plants. He will not even hesitate to chew wires, which can be very harmful for him. This is the reason why the rabbit needs to be supervised.

As an owner this can be uncomfortable and worrisome for you. But, you should know that this is absolutely normal for the bunny and that you can slowly train the Mini Rex Rabbit not to exhibit such behaviour. You can teach him to not bite you and others.

The first and foremost thing that you should remember is that you should not harm the pet when he tries to bite you. This could scare him and will make things worse for you. The pet needs to be handled with care if you wish to teach him the right behaviour in the household.

If you mishandle the pet and try to beat him up, he might also try to bite you and harm you. Avoid going down this road and aim at training the Mini Rex Rabbit well.

It is important that you understand the reason behind the Mini Rex Rabbit's biting. More often than not, Mini Rex Rabbits do so when they are in a playful mood.

If the Mini Rex Rabbit wants you to play with him, he could just signal you to do so by chewing. Such behaviour is quite common in younger Mini Rex Rabbits.

Another reason behind a Mini Rex Rabbit's nipping is that the animal could be scared. When you bring the pet to your home for the first time, everything around him will be new. It is quite natural for the pet to get scared. This is the reason that chewing and biting is very common in a new pet Mini Rex Rabbit.

When you know what you can expect from a new pet, it gets easier. Try to understand that he is still uncomfortable in the new surroundings and will require some time to get used to all that is new around him. Give him that space, time and also your understanding.

Biting comes very naturally to the Mini Rex Rabbits. But, this does not harm them because of the quality of their skin. If you notice the skin of your pet, you will find it to be very thick. This thick skin is a cushion for the Mini Rex Rabbit.

The Mini Rex Rabbit might be happy and playful, but his chewing and biting will hurt you, so it is important to train him against such behaviour.

As explained earlier, a Mini Rex Rabbit can exhibit such behaviour when they are scared. It should be noted that if the Mini Rex Rabbit has had a history of abuse, then you can expect him to chew and bite more in fear than in a playful mood.

If the Mini Rex Rabbit bites you hard you can have a really bad wound. This makes it all the more important to train the pet. There are many Mini Rex Rabbits that are beaten up and abused. If you have rescued one such animal, then you will definitely find him trying to bite you out of fear and tension.

But, don't worry because this is a passing phase. The love and warmth he will get at your place will help him to come out of his history of beatings and abuse.

If the pet is very young, he needs to be taught the behaviour that is expected of him. He needs to learn to be sociable. He needs to learn that it is not okay to bite people. There are some tips and tricks that will help you to teach him all this.

Every time the pet tries to bite you, you should loudly say the word 'no'. Do it each time, till the Mini Rex Rabbit starts relating the word 'no' to something that he can't do. Don't beat him because this will only scare him. Just be stern with your words and also actions.

If think that the above trick is not very useful, then you can put the pet in his cage for some time. The pet will eventually understand that this behaviour will send him into the cage. The word 'no' and the act of putting him into the cage will make the pet more cautious of his behaviour.

It should be noted that it will take some time for the Mini Rex Rabbit to understand this. Until then just be patient and keep repeating these actions each time he tries to nip you. The Mini Rex Rabbit will call back on his memory eventually and relate the cage to something punishable.

Another trick to help the Mini Rex Rabbit understand that he can't nip and bite is to hold him and drag him away from you. You need to establish the fact that you are the dominant one in the house.

When you are pulling the Mini Rex Rabbit away, you need to be very careful. You want to train the pet and not harm him. Use your thumb and the index finger to hold the skin at the back of the Mini Rex Rabbit's neck. This skin is loose and you will be able to hold it easily.

Look for the reactions of the Mini Rex Rabbit. He should not be in pain. The idea is to teach him to give up nipping and biting. When you hold him at the back of his neck, gently push him away from you.

You might have to repeat this action several times before the Mini Rex Rabbit understands what is expected of him. The Mini Rex Rabbit might also try to give you a good fight when you pull him away.

Don't worry because this is something normal and quite natural of the Mini Rex Rabbit. The Mini Rex Rabbits play and fight amongst themselves in the natural environment, so he might just try to defend and play with you.

There is another trick that can definitely help your training sessions with the Mini Rex Rabbit. You can apply something bitter on your toes and fingers, so that when the Mini Rex Rabbit bites you, he gets that bitter taste. When he tastes something bitter and terrible on you, he will eventually give up on nipping you.

It is important that the food item that you use is bitter but is not harmful for the Mini Rex Rabbit. You should know that there are some specially designed bitter foods for the Mini Rex Rabbits. These food items are prepared keeping in mind the training of the pet Mini Rex Rabbits.

You can easily buy these bitter food products online. You can also buy such products from the stores that have rabbit and bunny related stuff. You can buy various bitter products, such as bitter apple and bitter lemon.

These products are extremely safe for the Mini Rex Rabbit, so you can use them without any doubts. They render the bitter taste that will disgust the Mini Rex Rabbit. You just need to apply them or spray them to your toes and tips of the fingers. While you are working hard to train your pet Mini Rex

Rabbit well, you should remember that you don't want to do anything that is not right for the pet in the long run.

For example, if you use too much of these bitter food products, the digestive system of the Mini Rex Rabbit can get upset. You just need to spray a little. This will be enough to get the job done and also not affect the Mini Rex Rabbit in a negative way. He just needs a little to get the bitter taste in his mouth.

After your pet has tasted the bitter product and is disgusted, you need to make it up to him. Wash off your hands and toes nicely and give the pet a treat. This is important so that the pet is not scared of you and your hands. This will also make him realize that nipping is not accepted, but eating from your hands is.

There are many treats that the Mini Rex Rabbit can lick. You can find these treats online. You can also treat your pet to these foods, so that he can affectionately lick from your hands. You should remember that the Mini Rex Rabbit will start ignoring and avoiding you if he only gets to taste bitter stuff from you. Be a teacher to the pet, but remember to be a friendly teacher.

Another point that you need to know while training your pet is that you need to monitor your actions too. You need to figure out whether biting is a habit with the pet or has he suddenly started. If the pet has recently started biting, then it could be something related to you.

Another reason that could be behind your Mini Rex Rabbit's biting is that the Mini Rex Rabbit could be sick. You have to know your pet well to be able to detect sudden changes in his behaviour. If you see the pet being aggressive when you try to play with him, he could be sick.

You should thoroughly examine your pet for any injuries. If you spot an injury, you should take him to the veterinarian. If he looks sick and tired, even then it is a good idea to take him to the veterinarian. You should never postpone such things because this will drastically affect the pet's health.

4. Grooming the Mini Rex Rabbit

If you are domesticating the Mini Rex Rabbit for its fur or for showing the rabbit, then it is very important that you groom the pet nicely.

Grooming the pet rabbit is also necessary to maintain hygiene and well-being of the pet. Even if the pet will not participate in shows, you should make sure that he is neat and clean at all times.

When you are looking at grooming sessions for your Mini Rex Rabbit, you should pay special attention to the coat of the rabbit. This section will help you to understand the various dos and don'ts while grooming your pet Mini Rex Rabbit.

It should be noted here that the Mini Rex Rabbit will require frequent bathing. This is important to keep the fur in good condition. If you fail to groom the pet regularly, you will put the fur and the skin of the pet at risk.

When you decide to keep a Mini Rex Rabbit as a pet, you should understand that you will have to pay attention to the basic cleaning and grooming of the pet bunny.

Grooming is essential to keep the Mini Rex Rabbit clean and healthy. Not only will your rabbit appear neat and clean, he will also be saved from many unwanted diseases.

Mini Rex Rabbits are very calm by nature. This will allow you to groom the pet without much difficulty. They will not trouble you much, unlike many other pet animals.

The rabbit is easy to handle. Even when you give the Mini Rex Rabbit a bath, he will be calm and composed. This nature of the pet makes it very simple for the caregiver to bathe and groom the pet.

You should start the grooming sessions with the pet when he is very young. When you start a grooming session with the adult Mini Rex Rabbit, he might take some time to get used to the new routine.

On the other hand, if you start when the pet is very young, you give him some time to get accustomed to frequent grooming sessions. This is good for you and the pet in the long run.

You should take special care of the Mini Rex Rabbit's fur. The fur needs to be combed regularly to maintain the health and lustre of the same. If you don't comb it regularly, you will see the fur getting tangled.

Once the fur is tangled, it can be a real pain for you to get rid of these tangles. You will have to apply pressure and force, which can be very uncomfortable and painful for the pet Mini Rex Rabbit.

It is important to note that this can cause the bunny to shed loose tendrils of its fur. This is a warning signal for you as the caregiver of the pet that something is not right with the health of the Mini Rex Rabbit.

Mini Rex Rabbits have the tendency to groom themselves. They will lick themselves like cats. This can cause the bunny to swallow some of the hair or fur. The rabbit is unable to cough this ball of hair, like the cats.

This can lead to a serious health issue called wool block. The hairball remains inside the pet's body in this condition. This can lead to many complications if the condition is not treated on time.

The Mini Rex Rabbit feels that his stomach is full because of the presence of hairball in his stomach. This makes him lose his appetite and he eats less. This can be really detrimental for the overall health of the pet Mini Rex Rabbit.

You should help your pet in this condition by feeding large quantities of hay because it has fibre. You should also make sure that the pet Mini Rex Rabbit drinks a lot of water to help him during this condition.

Bathing the Mini Rex Rabbit

A Mini Rex Rabbit requires frequent bathing. It might be a difficult task for you to bathe your pet. But, this is no way means that it is okay for the bunnies to go without bathing. It is important that you schedule time for dedicated grooming and bathing of the Mini Rex Rabbit.

If the pet is not clean, he will attract fleas and other parasites. This only means extra work for you and veterinarian visits for the Mini Rex Rabbit. Make sure that the pet is well groomed to avoid other hassles.

To avoid the Mini Rex Rabbit from getting sick, make sure that the bunny is bathed every now and then. The frequency would depend on the climate and the environment of the bunny. If it is too hot or if the surroundings are not clean, it means that your pet should be given a bath more often.

Bathing is also important to keep the coat of the Mini Rex Rabbit clean. This is important to maintain good quality wool of the pet. If you don't clean the coat, the rabbit gets prone to many skin diseases.

If the Mini Rex Rabbit is shedding its tendrils, the excess fur might stick on to the body. When you give the pet a bath, the loose tendrils will just get washed off with water. This also means that the fur will not be shed all over the house.

When you are looking to give a nice bath to your Mini Rex Rabbit, you should be looking at two things, a good quality and mild shampoo and a few towels. It is very important that you choose the right shampoo for the Mini Rex Rabbit.

If the shampoo is too hard or harsh, it will leave rashes on the Mini Rex Rabbit and might even cause serious damage to his skin. This makes it important that you invest in buying a mild shampoo.

You can easily get a good quality shampoo online or in the pet store. Make sure that the shampoo that you choose is very mild on the skin and has proven to be ideal for the Mini Rex Rabbit.

You can take a small amount of shampoo and test it on a small part of the skin of the Mini Rex Rabbit. This is to make sure that the shampoo is safe for the pet. If you see the skin reacting, then you should make sure that you avoid this shampoo.

You also need a few towels handy for the Mini Rex Rabbit. They will help to dry the fur of the pet nicely. While one will be used to dry the water off, the others are required to cover the ground or floor.

The calm nature of the pet will make it easier for you to bathe him. But, there are a few precautions that you need to take. You should understand that how your rabbit behaves under water will depend on its individual personality.

It is important that you make a few attempts to understand your pet's personality. Don't give up and understand his behaviour and mannerisms. This will only help you in your future dealings with the pet.

If your Mini Rex Rabbit is suffering from a ringworm infestation, then you will have to use a shampoo that can help the Mini Rex Rabbit to get rid of the ringworms. You should consult the veterinarian before you use a specialized shampoo. It is important not to take a chance on the health of the Mini Rex Rabbit.

When you are ready to give the Mini Rex Rabbit a bath, you should make sure that the water you are using to bathe the pet is warm. The Mini Rex Rabbits should be bathed in warm water to keep them safe and warm.

Take a tub and fill it half with warm water. Make sure that the water is not too hot. You can keep this tub on a high platform. You can also keep it in the garden area. Make sure the surroundings are not too dusty and dirty.

Lift your pet animal delicately in your hands. Make sure that your grip is firm. To make sure that your grip is strong, place your hands on the stomach area and hold him firmly.

Place the Mini Rex Rabbit in the tub of warm water for a few seconds. Observe how he responds to water. If you see him enjoying, then your work becomes easier. You can also sprinkle water over the Mini Rex Rabbit.

Take him out of the water, and put some shampoo on his back. You should form a good lather with your hands from the ears towards the tail region. Make sure that the pet does not escape when you are shampooing it. You need to have a firm grip on him.

You need to make sure that the entire coat of the Mini Rex Rabbit is cleaned nicely. This is important so that the wool can be combed easily after the bath is done.

You can also make use of the kitchen sink to give the Mini Rex Rabbit a bath. You can fill the sink with water and use it. You can also keep talking to your pet to keep your pet entertained and busy.

Another way to bathe the bunny is to sway him under running warm water. Turn the tap on and make sure the water is warm. It should not be cold or too hot. Once you are convinced that the temperature of the water is right for the pet, hold the pet and bring him under the water for a few seconds.

Take him away from the water after a few seconds. Now apply some shampoo over the Mini Rex Rabbit. Keep swaying him under the water till all the shampoo is washed off. It is very important that all the shampoo is washed off. If there are shampoo residues on the pet's skin then the skin will get affected and will show signs of rashes and abrasions.

While you are bathing the Mini Rex Rabbit, it is important that you protect his face. Water should not enter his eyes or ears. These are sensitive areas and water could cause some damage to them.

Keep him on the towels and use another towel to pat him dry. Make sure that he is absolutely dry before you let him go, otherwise he will stick dust and dirt on his wool. You will have a hard time cleaning it then.

After the bath is done, place the Mini Rex Rabbit in a big towel. You should place a few blankets or towels on the floor to keep it warm and tight for the Mini Rex Rabbit. It is important that you are very gentle with the pet.

Once the pet Mini Rex Rabbit is dry, you should comb the fur of the bunny very nicely. This is important so that you can avoid any tangles. Once the tangles are formed, it will be very difficult to get rid of them.

You can also give green treats to your pet Mini Rex Rabbit during the bath session because you will be spending a lot of time bathing him. Though the pet is calm, he might get all worked up and fidgety after some time.

You can expect to spend about thirty to forty minutes in one bathing session with the Mini Rex Rabbit. It should be noted that that when the pet is shedding, the time will increase. You can expect to spend about forty to sixty minutes in one bathing session.

Grooming of nails, ears and teeth

The ears of the Mini Rex Rabbit need to be cleaned regularly so that there is no wax deposited in the ears. There are many owners who might not consider ear cleaning an important part of grooming, but in reality wax can lead to infections.

In severe cases, the hearing of the pet can be compromised. It is important that you know of the early signs of infestation. It is important to see the veterinarian in case you have a doubt about infestation.

Don't put any drops in the pet's ears without consulting the vet. In general, you should try to clean the Mini Rex Rabbit's ears once a week, or at least once in ten days.

You will require a cotton swab and an ear cleaning solution that will be easily available either online or at the store. If there is somebody in the house who could help you, it will be easier to clean the ears.

Sit comfortably on the floor and hold the bunny. Use your lap to give support to the bunny's legs. Take a cotton swab and apply some cleaning agent to it.

You should use the cotton swab with the cleaning agent to clean the parts of the ear that are easily visible to you. Don't go too deep because this can hurt the Mini Rex Rabbit.

You should definitely not try to go further in the ear canal. Repeat the process on both the ears. Do this process once in ten days to keep the ears clean.

The bunny might get uneasy and might try to get away from your grip. To make sure that the Mini Rex is stable and not jerking, you can give him a treat. This will keep Mini Rex Rabbit occupied and will make your job easier.

It is also important to cut the nails of the Mini Rex Rabbits regularly. You should be looking at doing so at least once a month. This is a part of overall grooming of the pet Mini Rex Rabbit. It needs to be done regularly.

You should also make sure that you use the right equipment to cut the nails of the pet Mini Rex Rabbit. You should good quality animal nail clippers. Along with that, you would need a soap and styptic powder.

If there is someone else in the house, you can ask them to hold the rabbit. This will make your job easier. But, even if there is no one, you can do it on your own. Place the pet animal in your lap in a way that he is comfortable and you have access to his nails.

If the nails of the bunny are not cut on a regular basis, there is a chance that the nails will get stuck somewhere. You can imagine the pain your bunny will have to go through if the nails are uprooted.

You will have to rush to the veterinarian to help the bunny. Not only this, the long nails can also leave marks and scratches on your skin. So, make it a point to cut the nails of the pet regularly.

As a rule, you should try to clean the bunny's teeth regularly. If you ignore his teeth, you will only invite unwanted problems for the pet Mini Rex Rabbit. You will notice tartar depositing on the teeth if they are not clean. This will automatically lead to decay of the teeth.

When you are considering the overall hygiene and cleanliness of the Mini Rex Rabbit, you also have to take care of his teeth. You might have problems cleaning the pet Mini Rex Rabbit's teeth in the beginning, but he will get used it very quickly.

Chapter 9: Showing the Mini Rex Rabbits

It is very important to train the animal to make him more suitable to a show. There are many owners that keep and domesticate Mini Rex Rabbits for the specific purpose of making them take part in shows. These shows are extensively popular amongst many rabbit lovers.

If you also wish to keep or domesticate the rabbit for the purpose of showing, then you need to make sure that you follow certain guidelines. The American rabbit breeders association has set some guidelines that will help you to prepare your Mini Rex to participate in such shows.

You should make sure that you understand these guidelines. These guidelines will help you not just in preparing your Mini Rex Rabbit for the show, but also to take good care of the pet. You will understand how to keep the pet in its best form.

This chapter will help you understand the various guidelines set by the American rabbit breeders association based on the specific Mini Rex breed. Follow these guidelines and present your Mini Rex in the best of its forms.

1. Guidelines for different breeds of Mini Rex Rabbits

The guidelines that you would follow for your bunny rabbit will depend on the breed of Mini Rex Rabbit you are domesticating. This section will help you understand the guidelines for various breeds of the Mini Rex Rabbits.

If you have the English Mini Rex Rabbit breed, then you must be in love with the facial furnishings of the animal. It is the only breed to of the Mini Rex to have the furnishings. This breed is known for its gentle behaviour.

The coat of English Mini Rex is very thick and lustrous. You should clean and brush it every single day if you wish to keep the coat in its best form. This is also necessary to avoid any tangles in the fur.

You should know that your rabbit will be judged mainly on the quality of its fur. You should make sure that it is in the best form possible.

When the English Mini Rex is made to participate in a show, the form of the rabbit would be judged. He should have a small and compact body. The look of the rabbit should remind one of a furry ball.

When it comes to the head of the rabbit, a dense coat of fur should surround the top and the side of the head. If this is not the case, then the Mini Rex would not be judged well for its health.

The French Mini Rex Rabbit breed should have guard hair. The under hair of the rabbit should be crimped. The fur needs to be strong and vibrant.

The Satin Mini Rex Rabbit should be of a medium built. The fur should be shiny and soft. The wool needs to be of a very good quality. The sheen of the wool should be visible.

The Giant Mini Rex Rabbit should have a commercial body type. The skin should be covered by a very dense coat of wool. The head should be oval and the trimmings should be clearly visible.

These are some guidelines that have been set and that are being followed by all the owners of the Mini Rex.

2. Preparing your Mini Rex Rabbit for the show

If you want to enter a show with your Mini Rex Rabbit, you will have to make sure that your rabbit is in its best form. You should take care of the health and well-being of the animal and make sure that he is ready for the contest.

After you are sure that your Mini Rex is ready to take part in the contest, you can plan on getting him admitted. You need to be a member of an organisation which will help you to contest.

The ARBA organisation and BRC organisation are the two organisations that will allow you to be a member and also enter a show with your Mini Rex Rabbit.

The process to become a member is fairly simple and straightforward. You need to approach the organisation and show an interest in being their member. You should also register your pet Mini Rex under your name.

Once you are a member of the organisation, you will be intimated with all the latest happenings and shows in your area. You should be alert regarding the requirements and deadlines.

Always keep checks on the shows happening in your area. You should check if your Mini Rex fits the requirements. When you find a show that allows your breed of Mini Rex Rabbit to take part in the contest, you should go ahead and register your Mini Rex Rabbit.

Register your Mini Rex Rabbit in the show that you find relevant and suitable. You will be asked your name, your address, breed, sex, age and colour of your bunny. You might also be asked whether you have taken part in contests before.

Once you have registered for the show, you need to make sure that you and the pet are ready. Make all the necessary arrangements to get to the venue much before the final day.

3. Fun tricks and games with the Mini Rex Rabbits

As the prospective owner of the Mini Rex Rabbit, you will be delighted to know that you can teach your pet Mini Rex Rabbit some fun games and tricks.

The way you can train your Mini Rex Rabbit for various essential things, you can also train them to understand some of your tricks. For example, the animal can be trained to know that he is being called.

You can teach him to associate certain actions with certain words. There are many other fun tricks that will help you bond with your pet. These tricks are also very entertaining. Your family and friends will surely have a great time when you and your pet do your fun tricks.

Like any other training, even these fun tricks will take some time. You will have to be patient with your pet if you want him to understand your commands well. There are some easy and fun tips that will make this process entertaining.

There are many tricks that you can teach the Mini Rex Rabbit. You can teach him to roll on the floor. Similarly, you can teach him to run around your feet when you command him to.

You can give a healthy treat to the pet when he is able to follow your instructions. The idea is to repeat a set of instructions and help him do an action.

Give him a treat when he does it right. This will help him to understand what is required of him. Treats are simple way of making the pets do what you want them to do.

In the beginning, you will have to repeat the set of instructions again and again. But, with the passage of time, your aim should be to reduce the number of times the instructions need to be repeated.

The pet bunny should be able to associate a set of words to an action. You should also not make him too dependent on the treats. This is not a very healthy thing to do.

It can be very difficult if the bunny hides and refuses to budge. Don't force him and give him some time. The Mini Rex Rabbits will follow your lead and will have fun with you, but you need to be a little patient with them.

A simple trick that you can try to make your pet bunny listen to you is to give him a special treat. All animals love treats. When he will see this favourite food item in your hand, he will get all excited.

When you bring the treat near him, take the treat upwards. The Mini Rex Rabbit will try to reach the treat, and in this process will stand on the hind legs.

Next, lower the treat towards the ground. The movement of the treat in your hand will also inspire the movement of the bunny. Do it every time you give him the treat.

You can also say the word dance when you move the treat upwards and downwards. The Mini Rex Rabbit will slowly realize that to eat the treat he will have to stand on the hind legs and then sit back.

Make sure you do this only for fun and not to trouble your pet Mini Rex Rabbit. Once you and your pet are good with the trick, you can flaunt and boast in front of your family and friends that you can make the pet perform tricks.

You can also teach your rabbit to do a certain action for you. But, this will take a lot of time and patience from you. For example, you can teach the pet to perform a roll over for you on the ground.

Lay the pet Mini Rex bunny on the ground, say the words roll over loud and clear and then give the pet a gentle roll over with your palm. Repeat this action many times. This will teach the pet that he needs to roll over.

The pet will start associating the word roll over with a roll over on the ground. When you say roll over, he will start rolling over on the ground on his own. This might take many days, even weeks of practice, so be prepared.

Also, if your pet seems uncomfortable with you rolling him over, you should just quit. Some bunnies might feel a little vulnerable with such an action. Understand your bunny's reactions and then take the next step.

These tricks and games can be very entertaining for everybody who gets to watch these tricks. Mini Rex Rabbits are anyways very entertaining and when you apply these simple tricks with them, they become more playful.

Conclusion

Thank you again for purchasing this book!

I hope this book was able to help you in understanding the various ways to domesticate and care for Mini Rex Rabbits.

Mini Rex Rabbits are cute, adorable, friendly and lovable animals. Even though they are loved as pets, there are still many doubts regarding their domestication methods and techniques. There are many things that the prospective owners don't understand about the animal. They find themselves getting confused as to what should be done and what should be avoided.

A Mini Rex Rabbit is a small and naughty animal that will keep you busy and entertained by all its unique antics and mischiefs. It is said that each animal is different from the other. Each one will have some traits that are unique to him. It is important to understand the traits that differentiate the bunny from other animals. You also have to be sure that you can provide for the animal. So, it is important to be acquainted with the dos and don'ts of keeping the Mini Rex Rabbit.

If you are still contemplating whether you want to domesticate the Mini Rex or not, then it becomes all the more important for you to understand everything regarding the pet very well. You can only make a wise decision when you are acquainted will all these and more. When you are planning to domesticate a Mini Rex Rabbit as a pet, you should lay special emphasis on learning about its behaviour, habitat requirements, diet requirements, breeding details and common health issues.

When you decide to domesticate an animal, it is important that you understand the animal and its species well. It is important to learn the basic nature and mannerisms of the animal. This book will help you to equip yourself with this knowledge. You will be able to appreciate the bunnies for what they are. You will also know what to expect from the animal. This will help you to decide whether the rabbit is the right choice for you or not. If you already have a Mini Rex Rabbit, then this book will help you to strengthen your bond with your pet.

The ways and strategies discussed in the book are meant to help you get acquainted with everything that you need to know about Mini Rex Rabbits. You will be able to understand the unique antics of the animal. This will help you to decide whether the Mini Rex Rabbit is suitable to be your pet or not.

You will be surprised to see how friendly and lovable these animals are, once you make attempts to take care of them.

The book teaches you simple ways that will help you to understand your pet, and also give it all the care and comfort they need as pets. This will allow you to take care of your pet in a better way. You should be able to appreciate your pet and also care well for the animal with the help of the techniques discussed in this book. You should be able to improve the quality of the rabbit's life as your pet with the help of this book.

Thank you and good luck!

References

https://en.wikipedia.org

http://www.nationalgeographic.com

www.ehow.co.uk

http://www.runningbugfarm.com

http://joyofhandspinning.com

http://www.mini Rexrabbits.co.za

http://www.rabbit.org

http://www.mnn.com

http://www.handallhousefarm.com

http://www.mainemini Rexproducers.com

http://twotalentshomestead.blogspot.in

http://www.raising-rabbits.com

http://www.mini Rexfiber.com

https://joybileefarm.com

http://www.wikihow.com

https://www.thespruce.com

https://www.pets4homes.co.uk

http://www.hobbyfarms.com

www.bbc.co.uk

https://www.cuteness.com

www.training.ntwc.org

http://animaldiversity.org

https://a-z-animals.com

https://www.theguardian.com

http://www.businessinsider.com

https://hub.co-opinsurance.co.uk

https://www.popsugar.com

http://ipfactly.com

https://www.petcha.com

http://www.petrabbitinfo.com

https://www.peta2.com/news/mini Rex-bunnies-facts/

Lightning Source UK Ltd.
Milton Keynes UK
UKHW022217070920
369495UK00010B/2387